This book is dedicated to my uncles, John Baily and Eamon Heaney, who took me to my first games at Anfield and Goodison Park.

First published 1993   The Bluecoat Press
Bluecoat Chambers
School Lane
Liverpool L1 3BX

Designed by: MARCH design

Printed by: Printeksa

ISBN 1 872568 11 4

Front cover photograph by Barry Farrell.
Back cover photograph by Steve Hale

SHANKLY

Phil Thompson

THE BLUECOAT PRESS

Finney and Shankly in action at Gerry Byrne's testimonial match at Anfield.

Foreword
by Tom Finney

THE legend of Bill Shankly is known and respected the footballing world over and I was lucky enough to meet him in his prime as a player and watch his genius unfold in later years as a manager.

Although he was a colleague with Preston North End, it was really as a ruthless and talented manager with Liverpool that Bill became a football great. Wherever he played, managed, visited or just talked about the game, Bill was infectious, fanning the flames of public interest. He recognised the might of his Liverpool challenge from day one and turned a passionate, football-crazy city into a world force. Cup followed cup and he retained dignity and charm throughout his incredible success.

Basically, even allowing for his sharp wit and Scottish humour, Bill was a quiet, shy and humble man, soon embarrassed by the limelight. But this attitude and enthusiasm towards football made him a great example for the likes of the young Finney joining the professional ranks at Deepdale some fifty-five years ago. You could not fail to be impressed by his efforts, whether on the training ground or in match action; he never gave less than his best. Defeat never came into any discussion, he could not stand the thought of losing. A great motivator, he often got ordinary players performing beyond their capabilities, making them believe they were better than they thought. No player of Shankly's ever shirked a challenge or hid from his responsibilities. Every man Jack went out there with a job to do and did it - or else.

The stories about Shanks are limitless, but I remember one back in 1960 when he turned out for my testimonial as a member of an invited all stars, which also included Trautmann, Franklin, Wright, Matthews, Mortensen, Lofthouse, Liddell and so on. A few days prior to the game I received a call from Bill who was 47 at the time. I had decided that, allowing for Bill's age, his involvement should be to run the line. When I told him he very nearly blew a gasket, 'Son, you must be bloody joking, I am coming to play for the full 90 minutes and that's the end of it.' Keen as mustard, totally indignant and still making decisions for me - what a fellow - I loved him!

Tom Finney

From Glenbuck
To Preston

BILL SHANKLY was born on September 2, 1913, in the coal-mining village of Glenbuck, Ayrshire. At the time of his birth, the population of Glenbuck was declining and totalled about six hundred people. This was a time when it was becoming increasingly difficult to obtain good quality coal from the local mines and it led to a gradual exodus from Glenbuck to the nearby villages, where a better quality of coal and prospects of more stable employment were available.

On leaving school at the age of fourteen, it was inevitable that Bill would begin work at the nearby pit and it was an experience that would affect him deeply. His first job at the pit was sorting out the coal from the stones and then returning the empty truck back down the pit. He would earn extra money on a Sunday emptying coal wagons with a shovel at a rate of sixpence a ton. All of this work took place at the pit top but, within six months, he was sent to work at the pit bottom. Here, for the first time, he experienced the full horror of what it was like to work as a miner during the days before nationalization drastically improved their lot. Health and safety were not at a premium and the stench of damp, lack of ventilation and atrocious conditions that the miner had to work in were never forgotten by Shankly. Although he did acknowledge that conditions improved for them during the post-war years, he knew the struggle that the miners had to go through to achieve better working conditions and throughout his life he had great sympathy with their plight.

After a two year period working underground, the pit was closed and Shankly was made redundant. For the first time in his life, Shankly had to sign on the dole. With the prospect of employment in Glenbuck and its nearby areas virtually non-existent, Shankly spent his time walking or, if he had any spare money, playing cards. He even helped out his sister Elizabeth with her paper round.

Bill was the youngest in a family of five boys and five girls. As was the case with the majority of working class boys in Britain during this period, football was an obsession in the village. It can be said that football was literally in the blood of the Shankly family with Bill's mother, Barbara, having two brothers

Opposite: Shankly tackles Lishman of Arsenal at Highbury, 1949.

who were professional footballers. Bob Blyth played for Rangers, Middlesborough, Preston, Dundee and Portsmouth and Bill Blyth played for Preston and Carlisle. It was no surprise, therefore, that as soon as they were old enough to kick a ball, the Shankly boys came under the spell of football and practised and played the game constantly. The fact that all five of them went on to become professional footballers was an incredible achievement. Alec, the oldest boy, was the first to sign professional terms and played for Ayr United and Clyde. The rest of the Shankly boys followed suit with James playing for Portsmouth, Halifax, Coventry, Carlisle, Sheffield United, Southend United and Barrow; John playing for Portsmouth, Luton, Blackpool, Alloa and Morton; Bob playing for Alloa, Tunbridge Wells and Falkirk; and finally, Bill who played for Carlisle United and Preston North End.

Sporting prowess was not restricted to Barbara's side of the family, however. Bill's father, John, who worked originally as a postman and then as a bespoke tailor, was a quarter-mile runner of some note. John Shankly played football only during his school days but always maintained a high level of fitness.

Life was not easy for Barbara and John Shankly and bringing up their five sons and five daughters (Netta, Elizabeth, Isobel, Barbara and Jean) on very little money was later described by Bill as a miracle. Like his son, John did not smoke or drink but loved to go to the cinema. It was an eight mile round trip to the nearest one but John would often make the journey on foot to watch a movie.

John Shankly was known as an honest, straight-talking man. Barbara was a woman who, though she had little, would share what she had with anyone. It was these characteristics of his parents that were ingrained in Bill and helped to mould a man who would be idolised by many thousands, as much for the warmth and uniqueness of his personality as for his incredible ability as a football manager.

Shankly was offered a trial with his famous village team, Glenbuck Cherrypickers, but was considered too young at sixteen to join them. Within a year, the Cherrypickers had folded and Shankly never had the chance to represent his village.

Shankly began to display his notable football prowess after this with local junior team Cronberry. It was here that he learned how to look after himself, playing with and against men many years his senior. He was always keen to point out that although it was called junior football, it was junior in name only: there was no age limit and he would often come up against experienced men who played the game hard. It was also whilst at Cronberry that a scout recommended him to Bill Blyth, a director at Carlisle and, of course, Shankly's uncle, who was a key figure in the development of the all-action half-back. Shankly was invited to Brunton Park for trials.

On his first trip out of Scotland Bill, seventeen at the time, was accompanied to Carlisle by his brother Alec. After his trial match on August 20 and just one game, a reserve match against Middlesborough Reserves on August 27, 1932, which Carlisle lost 6-0, Shankly had shown enough promise to warrant an offer of professional terms with Carlisle. He was initially on a month's trial but was soon signed up for the rest of the season and, thankfully, his brief taste of unemployment was at an end. Guided by trainer Tommy Curry and team-manager Tom Hampson, Shankly forced himself into the first team. Becoming a professional allowed Shankly to train even harder; his objective being that one should be fit enough to play flat out for not ninety minutes but one hundred and twenty minutes.

Shankly played regularly for the Reserves through the rest of 1932 and, on December 31, made his full league debut for Carlisle against Rochdale, which ended in a 2-2 draw. He played sixteen games over the rest of the season, all at right-half, and by April a local newspaper commented that 'Shankly is a most promising player. He is attracting attention!' At the end of the 1932-33 season, Carlisle finished in 19th place and many of the team received free transfers; Shankly, however, was offered and signed a new contract.

After a happy season learning his trade at Carlisle, Shankly travelled home to Glenbuck content with life and looking forward to the summer break. He was by now a first team regular and was being paid a weekly wage of four pounds ten shillings to play a game that he would gladly have played for nothing. When he compared his occupation with that of the miner, he knew he was well off. Shankly later recalled his thoughts at the time:

For as long as I can remember my sole aim in life was to play football. When I worked down the pit in Scotland, all I dreamed about was the end of the shift and legging it to the nearest field for a game.

Shankly's close season break was brought to an abrupt end when a telegram arrived at his family home from Carlisle United. It instructed him to report back to Brunton Park the following day but gave no other hint of what he was being summoned back to Carlisle for. Once again, Alec accompanied his younger brother and, on their arrival at Carlisle, Shankly's Uncle Bill informed him that a Preston North End representative, Bill Scott, was waiting to speak to him. Before introducing Scott, Blyth revealed that Preston had made a five hundred pound offer to Carlisle for Bill Shankly's services for the coming season. They were also willing to offer a personal payment of sixty pounds and a wage of five pounds a week. At first, Shankly turned the offer down: he was happy at Carlisle and the wages Preston were offering were little more than he was already receiving. A disappointed Bill Scott trooped out of Brunton Park, unhappy that he had failed to lure the young Scottish player to the Lancashire club.

As soon as Scott had left the room, Alec got to work on Bill, explaining that Preston were once a great team and were capable of becoming so again. It was an opportunity that should be taken. Convinced by Alec's powers of reasoning, the two brothers set off to catch up with Scott, who had by this time departed Carlisle to catch the Newcastle train. They caught up with him just as he was boarding the train and quickly jumped on as it pulled out of the station. Bill explained to a delighted Scott that he would be pleased to join Preston North End and, after signing the appropriate forms, the Shankly brothers alighted the train at the next station and returned to Carlisle. For five hundred pounds, Preston had captured a player who would give them loyal service for the next sixteen years.

Shankly's last appearance for Carlisle was at home for the Reserves against Wallsend on May 5, 1933; a match which, incidentally, ended in a 6-0 win for Carlisle.

On hearing news of the sale of Shankly to Preston, Carlisle United's supporters were up in arms but their protests were to no avail and, in July 1933, Shankly reported for pre-season training at Deepdale for the first time. Reports in the Preston newspapers of North End's capture of the promising teenage half-back were low key. There was little hint that they had, in fact, signed a player whom they would soon be describing as 'a human dynamo' and 'an iron man'.

Shankly began his Preston career with a debut for the reserve team in the Central League against Blackpool Reserves. He started with a victory and within a few months had been promoted to the first team. His first team debut was against Hull City and Preston ran out comfortable 5-0 winners.

Shankly's first season at Deepdale was a momentous one, with Preston regaining a place in the First Division as runners-up to Second Division champions, Grimsby Town. Preston North End football correspondent at the time, Walter Pilkington, was clearly impressed with Shankly's first season at the club and in his end of season notes he wrote:

One of this season's discoveries, Bill Shankly, played with rare tenacity and uncommonly good ideas for a lad of twenty. He is full of good football and possessed with unlimited energy; he should go far.

Pilkington also revealed a conversation with Shankly that displayed the ambitions of the young Scot. He recalled:

I was returning by train from a match at Plymouth in a 'sleeper', with Bill Shankly and Jimmy Dougal as bunk companions. I asked Bill what he wanted most. 'To play for Scotland, sir' he replied, without a moment's hesitation.

As with football management, it took Shankly a few years to achieve his objective but his international ambitions were finally realised when he was selected to represent Scotland against England at Wembley, in 1938. Before achieving international honours, however, Shankly had the task of helping Preston consolidate their hard won position back in the First Division. This was achieved with the minimum of fuss and, by the late 1930s, Preston had developed a team that were capable of holding their own against the best in the land.

In 1937 Shankly achieved what had been a dream since his days kicking a ball around the village football pitch in Glenbuck: to play in an FA Cup Final at Wembley. After victories against Newcastle, Stoke, Exeter, Spurs and West Brom, Preston were through to their first Cup Final since losing to Huddersfield Town in the 1922 Final held at Stamford Bridge. They had won through to Wembley with a goal aggregate of 19 for and 6 against and their form leading up to the Final appeared to give them the edge over their opponents, Sunderland. The fact that it had taken Sunderland a total of eight hard fought matches to get to Wembley was another factor in Preston's favour and they stepped out at Wembley in confident mood.

As the two teams lined up to face each other on May Day, 1937, they became the first players to participate in a May Cup Final. Prior to this date, the FA Cup Final was traditionally played on the last Saturday in April. As part of the celebrations to mark the coronation of King George VI, however, the Football Association decided to move the Final to the first Saturday in May. King George and Queen Elizabeth were both present on what was a perfect, early summer's day.

It was Preston who were looking the most dangerous from the start. Prompted by half-backs Shankly and Milne (father of future Preston, Liverpool and England star, Gordon Milne) Preston kept up the pressure on Sunderland and it was no surprise when O'Donnell latched on to a pass from Dougal and blasted the ball past Mapson in the Sunderland goal. In twelve of the previous Finals, the team that had scored first at Wembley had gone on to win the Cup and Preston were confident it was to be their day.

If the first half had been all Preston, the second saw a dramatic turnaround, with Sunderland taking total control of the game. Gurney scored an equaliser and Raich Carter, who even then was acknowledged as one of the all-time greats, scored a breathtaking goal to put them into the lead.

With nineteen minutes left, Carter glided past full-back Gallimore, before slotting the ball past Preston keeper Burns. Sunderland's fantastic comeback was completed six minutes later when a sweeping move involving Gurney, Gallacher and Burbanks resulted in Burbanks sealing Preston's fate with a fine finish past the bemused Preston goalkeeper. In later years, Shankly admitted that they were beaten by a far superior team on the day. In many ways the Sunderland team of 1937 played the same brand of 'total football' as the great Holland team of the 1970s, with full-backs Gorman and Hall leading many of their attacks that developed from every section of the team. Shankly once stated that it was a frightening experience to visit Roker Park during the late 1930s because Sunderland were such a terrific outfit.

The following season, 1937-38, was also memorable in many ways for Shankly and his Preston team. He won his much coveted first Scottish cap and scored his first league goal, on February 2, 1938, against Liverpool. Preston were narrowly pipped in a close race for the league championship and Shankly returned to Wembley to help his team defeat Huddersfield Town 1-0 in another eventful final.

It was a joyous day for Shankly and his family back home in Glenbuck when news came through that he had been selected to make his international debut on April 9, 1938 against the old enemy, England, at Wembley. Preston, in fact, had four of their players in the Scotland team that day: Bill Shankly, Andy Beattie, Tom Smith and George Mutch. The impact of the Scottish players on the Preston teams of the late 1930s can be gauged from the fact that their 1936 line-up included no less than nine Scots: Shankly, Milne, Beattie, Dougal, Maxwell, Smith, Fagan, F. O'Donnell and H. O'Donnell. It was little wonder that they were known at the time as the 'Preston Scottish'.

The call up of Shankly to the Scotland team began a succession of half-backs who would represent their country with an infectious spirit and passion. After Shankly came Scoular, Evans, Docherty and MacKay. All were great half-backs who had a touch of steel about their play.

Preston's international half-back.

BILL SHANKLY.

The England team that took the field against Scotland was quite a formidable line-up and within minutes of the start of the match, Shankly was welcomed to international football by a tackle from England's Wilf Copping that ripped through his shin guard, causing an ugly gash on his leg. The older Copping was determined to make his mark on Shankly as early as possible and this he did, literally! Never one to complain, Shankly played on and helped the Scots to a 1-0 victory, the winning goal being scored by Hearts player, Tommy Walker.

Arsenal's hard man, Copping, once again inflicted a painful injury on Shankly during a league game later in Shankly's career. In his autobiography, Shankly admitted he was sad when he heard of Copping's retirement from football, for he had been biding his time waiting for the opportunity to return the compliment.

Two weeks after his international debut, Shankly was back at Wembley to face Huddersfield in the 1938 FA Cup Final. Although the match was not a classic, the events of the last minute of the game resulted in it being a Cup Final that is argued over to this day. Once again Preston were installed as

Shankly being introduced to King George VI before the 1938 FA Cup Final.

favourites by the bookies and were confidently expected to be too strong for their Yorkshire opponents. Preston had been strongly fancied to land the league championship all season and it was only at the death that Arsenal took the title, with Wolves runners-up and Preston finishing a close third. In contrast, Huddersfield had been struggling in the lower reaches of the table and had finished in nineteenth position.

The first ninety minutes of the game, the first ever to be broadcast live in its entirety with an estimated 10,000 television viewers following the play, failed to produce a goal. For the first time, extra time was played at Wembley and, prompted by the tireless Shankly, Preston were looking the most likely to break the deadlock. With the game entering the last minute of extra time, Shankly fed a ball through to George Mutch. The Preston danger man began to move menacingly towards the Huddersfield penalty area. Alf Young, the Huddersfield centre-half and captain, who until this moment had been having an inspired game in the Town defence, thrust out a leg in a desperate attempt to stop Mutch. The Preston forward tumbled to the ground and the referee, Jimmy Jewell, judging the challenge illegal, pointed to the spot.

After failing to entice any of his team-mates, including the normally ice-cool Shankly, to take on the responsibility of deciding the fate of the FA Cup,

Above: The victorious Preston team parade around Wembley with the FA Cup, 1938.
Opposite, above: George Mutch scores the extra time winner from the penalty spot in the 1938 FA Cup Final. Note that the white paint from the ball's impact with the crossbar can clearly be seen.
Opposite, below: George Mutch's extra time winner against Huddersfield, 1938.

Mutch brushed himself down before stepping up to take the penalty that would decide the match. A hush came over Wembley as Mutch ran up and blasted the ball with as much power as he could muster. The shot crashed against the bar before rolling over the line and into the net, leaving the disconsolate Huddersfield keeper, Hesford, sprawling helplessly on the lush turf. The Preston supporters erupted as Mutch was mobbed by his team-mates, delirious in the knowledge that the Cup was returning to Preston for the first time this century. Alf Young, the man who had conceded the penalty, was in tears as the final whistle blew. As his team mates consoled the sad and dejected figure, the Preston captain, Tom Smith, strode up to the Royal Box to collect the Cup from King George.

To this day, Huddersfield supporters maintain that photographic evidence suggests that the foul was committed outside the penalty area but, nonetheless, history books tell us that a George Mutch penalty won the FA Cup for Preston in 1938 and the match ball still has the white paint on it from its contact with the newly painted crossbar.

To be part of an FA Cup winning team at Wembley was always considered by Shankly to be the biggest thrill of his football career. When asked later about the penalty incident, he expressed no doubts:

Of course it was a penalty. It's a terrible thing when a man has nothing left to do but bring another man down. I was standing next to Alf Young afterwards. Tears were running down his cheeks. I said to him, 'Ay, and that's no' the first one you've given away!'

Captain of Scotland during a wartime international.

The War Years

THE outbreak of war in 1939 saw Bill Shankly enlist in the RAF. He approached the services as he approached his life, doing everything he was asked to the best of his ability. He was careful to maintain his high level of fitness and would run the lanes and countryside of wherever he was posted. After being stationed at Padgate and then St Athan, in South Wales, he was sent to a camp in Manchester. Manchester suited Shankly perfectly, with regular football and boxing available. While there, he played soccer in the Manchester and District League and won a cup boxing for his camp at middle-weight and was also selected for his second wartime international, being picked to play against England.

When the news came through that he was being posted to Arbroath for a junior NCO's course, Shankly was very disappointed. He had enjoyed his stay at Manchester to such an extent and made friends with so many people that he did not want to leave. After further postings to Great Yarmouth and then Henlow in Bedfordshire, Shankly was finally stationed in Glasgow for the duration of the war.

While stationed at the various camps, Shankly took every opportunity to guest for the local league clubs, who always seemed to get word of when an international player was stationed nearby. Many servicemen, including Shankly, would risk 'jankers' to turn out when there was no weekend pass for them.

Shankly played three games under the name of Newman for Norwich in January, 1943. In the first of these, against an army XI, he scored twice in an 8-4 win for the home team, with the attendance recorded as 484. Whenever possible, clubs protected players who were chancing getting caught for being absent without leave. Team line-ups would not be released until a week or two after the match had taken place. Apart from helping players to keep up a decent standard of match fitness, the small amount of extra cash that the players received in match fees and expenses was a valuable addition to their service pay. An example of the amount that players received can be gauged from Shankly's thirty shillings (£1.50) fee that he received from Cardiff City after playing for them against Lovells Athletic, in 1942.

Apart from Norwich, Shankly played for Preston, Liverpool, Arsenal, Luton, Cardiff, Bolton, East Fife and Partick Thistle during the war years. Highlights of Shankly's wartime football career were the 1941 War Cup Final against Arsenal at Wembley, which Preston won after a replay and captaining Scotland in a wartime international.

After playing in nearly every game for Arsenal during one of the wartime Cup competitions, Shankly was rather aggrieved to be dropped for the Final against Charlton at Wembley. Arsenal had most of their players available for the game and Shankly was not selected for the Final, their own registered players taking precedence. Shankly regarded this as an injustice and, despite Arsenal's attempts to placate him with a cash and ticket payment, the dejected Scot trooped out of Highbury handing back the 'sweetener' on his way out. Shankly made a mental note that if he were ever in a position to select a team in the future, it would be solely on ability, with sentiment never allowed into the equation. Joe Mercer remembered the incident when interviewed in the 1970s. He recalled:

He would get terribly upset over injustices and matters of principle. I remember one day he was terribly worked up. He played for Arsenal during the war and I met him outside Wembley when they played Charlton in a wartime Cup Final. Bill had played right through the competition but George Male had arrived home and they picked him instead of Bill. He was most indignant and his language was dreadful.

Shankly, in fact, decided to stand on the terraces to watch the game, which Arsenal won 7-1.

Shankly's posting to Glasgow was to prove a happy and eventful period in his life. It was while stationed there that he met his future wife, Nessie, who was in the WRAF at the same camp. Nessie first spotted Bill jogging around the camp and, knowing nothing about football, made enquiries about the strange man who appeared to be permanently training. The information that he was Bill Shankly, a famous international footballer, meant little to her but within a short period of time they got to know each other and, in 1944, they married in Nessie's home town of Glasgow. In his autobiography, Shankly revealed that he would often woo Nessie with toasted cheese that he took over from his section to hers.

In later years, when Bill moved to football management, the Shankly family had to undergo a considerable amount of upheaval, moving from one area of the country to another as Shankly changed jobs in the management merry-go-round before settling on Merseyside. Whatever career move Bill made, it was with the full support of Nessie, who always provided a strong and stable family environment while allowing her husband to devote an enormous amount of his time and energy into building and developing whatever football club was receiving his service at the time.

While stationed in Glasgow, Shankly signed to play for Partick Thistle and, apart from providing him with a good standard of football, he was eternally grateful to them for paying all expenses when he had an operation on his knee. It was an injury that Shankly had been carrying for some time but to him injuries did not exist and he had chosen to ignore it. The medical attention he finally succumbed to revealed that he had been playing for a long period of time with a badly displaced cartilage. In his later years as a manager, he demanded this same level of courage and toughness from his players and, as Gerry Byrne's incredible FA Cup Final display against Leeds, in 1965, showed, he usually got it. After regaining his fitness, Shankly continued to play for Partick Thistle until he was demobbed in January, 1946.

Shankly's first game on his return to Preston was an FA Cup tie against Everton that was to be played over two legs. Shankly won the game for Preston with an extra time penalty kick at Goodison Park. Although finishing the season without honours, the North End faithful were richly entertained by a player Shankly regarded as a football genius, Tom Finney. Nicknamed the 'Preston Plumber', Finney's game did not have a weakness. He was skilful with both feet, strong in a tackle and a brilliant header of the ball. Finney is regarded by many soccer pundits as the only genuine challenger to George Best as the greatest all-round soccer talent of the post-war years in Britain. Later, Shankly would never tire from telling his players at Liverpool about the great Tom Finney: *'He was so good that the opposition would have a man*

marking him in the pre-match warm up!' And if any of his Liverpool players got a little bit too big for their boots, Shankly would soon bring them down a notch with a curt *'Tom Finney could play better than you with his overcoat on!'*

If Finney made an immediate impression on Shankly, the feeling was mutual, with the young Preston player being particularly struck by Shankly's incredible enthusiasm and will to win. During Finney's home debut for Preston, he remembers being constantly urged by Shankly to *'keep on trying, we can still win.'* The fact that Preston were four down with just a few minutes to play meant nothing to the indomitable Scot. Within a short period, Finney's talent made him a marked man, with opposing defenders trying every trick in the book, including threats of physical violence. On one occasion, Shankly overheard a seasoned professional threatening Finney with a broken leg. Shankly sidled up to the player in question and in no uncertain terms told him that if he broke Finney's leg, then Shankly would break his. With Shankly's ultimatum in mind, the player had second thoughts and did not bother Finney again for the rest of the game.

The late 1940s saw Shankly playing his final couple of seasons for Preston, who were still regarded as one of the most entertaining teams in the country. After a defeat at Highbury, which saw league leaders Arsenal increase their

21

Left: Match programme for Everton v Preston North End, 1936-37.

Right: Match programme Liverpool v Preston, 1947-48. Two future Liverpool legends, Shankly and Paisley, come face to face.

FIRST DIVISION LEAGUE MATCH

Everton v. Preston N. E.

AT GOODISON PARK.   KICK-OFF 2-30 p.m.

RIGHT   EVERTON   LEFT

(Colours: Royal Blue Jerseys; White Knickers with Blue Stripe down Seams)

SAGAR

2   COOK   3   JONES

4   6

BRITTON   GEE   MERCER

7   8   9   10   11

GILLICK   CUNLIFFE   DEAN   STEVENSON   LEYFIELD

Referee: Linesmen:

Mr. J. RENNIE   Mr. E. C. ROBINSON, Blue & White Flag

(Oldham)   Mr. J. H. IRVING, Red & White Flag.

O'DONNELL, H.   FAGAN   O'DONNELL, F.   BERESFORD   DOUGAL

12   13   14   15   16

MILNE   SMITH   SHANKLY

17   18   19

LOWE   GALLIMORE, F.

20   21

HOLDCROFT

22

LEFT   PRESTON N. E.   RIGHT

(Colours: White Jerseys; Dark Blue Knickers)

N.B.—Team changes will be recorded at side of Score Board.

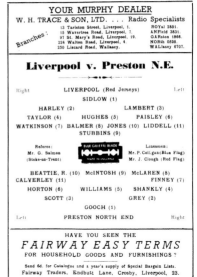

Liverpool v. Preston N.E.

Right   LIVERPOOL (Red Jerseys)   Left

SIDLOW (1)

HARLEY (2)   LAMBERT (3)

TAYLOR (4)   HUGHES (5)   PAISLEY (6)

WATKINSON (7) BALMER (8) JONES (10) LIDDELL (11)

STUBBINS (9)

Referee: Linesmen:

Mr. G. Salmon   Mr. P. Colligan (Blue Flag)

(Stoke-on-Trent)   Mr. J. Clough (Red Flag)

BEATTIE, R. (10)   McINTOSH (9)   McLAREN (8)

CALVERLEY (11)   FINNEY (7)

HORTON (6)   WILLIAMS (5)   SHANKLY (4)

SCOTT (3)   GREY (2)

GOOCH (1)

Left   PRESTON NORTH END   Right

lead over third placed Preston in February, 1948, Preston chairman, James Taylor, a man Shankly greatly admired, commented: *'I don't mind if we lose so long as the team serves up first class football!'*

Shankly's incredible fitness impressed Edgar Turner of the Sporting Chronicle who, after witnessing the Preston Captain, now well into his thirties, clinch a victory over Chelsea at Deepdale, commented:

It was human dynamo Bill Shankly who scored Preston's second from the penalty spot. How Shankly keeps it up game after game, year after year, I don't know. He's been with Preston fifteen seasons now and is playing as well as ever.

Speaking to the Sporting Chronicle, in 1948, after playing his 290th league game for Preston, Shankly rejected rumours that he was about to retire when he told John Graydon:

I'd be grateful, John, if you would deny a report that I'm thinking of retiring. Some people seem to think I'm a veteran because I have been playing for many seasons. I'm only 34, and you don't call that old, do you? I intend to go on playing as long as possible and my great ambition is to captain Preston at Wembley.

Graydon backed up Shankly's statement that he was far from finished by citing a recent game against Arsenal, after which Graydon wrote:

On his form against Arsenal, Bill Shankly, with Archie MacCauley and Arsenal's Joe Mercer, again showed how to play artistic football without wasting energy, and many of Shankly's along-the-carpet passes might have brought goals had Preston had a more forceful centre-forward.

Shankly's wish to captain Preston at Wembley looked like it would be fulfilled in 1948 when a McIntosh goal against Manchester City at Maine Road gave them a quarter-final game, again at Maine Road, against Manchester United. Preston, under the guidance of Shankly and Bobbie Beattie, their two most experienced campaigners, were confident that this was their year for the FA Cup. However, Manchester United, under the inspired captaincy of Johnny Carey, knocked Preston out and went on to win the Cup that year.

The following season, 1948-49, was to be Shankly's last at the Lancashire club. No longer able to command a regular first team place, Shankly was on the lookout for a new opportunity in football and, despite his previous claims that he was not thinking of retiring from the playing side, it had always been obvious, particularly amongst his peers, that Shankly was prime managerial material. With Preston struggling to avoid relegation, Shankly was brought back into the team during the early months of 1949. With star player Finney suffering a series of injuries that kept him out of the team that season, Preston were fighting a losing battle to retain their First Division status.

Early Managerial Career

WORD that Shankly was looking for a new opportunity reached Third Division Carlisle United, who were keen to fill the managerial vacancy at the club with a young 'track suit' manager. After meeting the Carlisle board, the Cumbrian club offered their ex-player his first managerial position. They also offered wages that were the equivalent of what he was receiving at Preston and, coupled with the fact that Carlisle was only a few hours from Glasgow, which would allow Nessie to see her family in Scotland more often, the offer to take over at Carlisle held considerable appeal to Shankly.

When he informed Preston of his decision, they did not react favourably. Although he was no longer a first team regular, they were obviously keen to hang on to all of their experienced players in their fight against relegation. A benefit game was offered as an incentive to stay but Shankly, after giving the club sixteen years of loyal service, was under the impression that a benefit match would be awarded to him regardless of whether he stayed with the club or not.

The dilemma for Shankly was that if he did not accept the managerial opportunity that had presented itself, another might not emerge for a long time. He decided to stand by his decision to leave Preston but was embittered by the fact that a benefit match was no longer on offer.

Up to this point, Shankly had regarded joining Preston in 1933 as the greatest football decision of his life and could not have been happier. Although his departure from Preston had not been as amicable as he had hoped, it was not a rift that lasted for any great length of time (as Shankly's dealings in the transfer market with the Deepdale club in the 1960s will bear out). Just as Shankly's name as a manager would always be synonymous with Liverpool FC, Shankly's playing career will always be intrinsically linked to Preston North End. Just three matches short of his 300th league game for Preston, Shankly played his final game for them on March 19, 1949, against Sunderland at Deepdale. A notable record that Shankly created at Preston was 43 successive FA Cup ties for one club.

Although Shankly accepted the Carlisle post on March 22, contractual difficulties with Preston still had to be sorted out and his first game in charge at Carlisle was not until April 4, which was the Cumberland Cup Final against Workington, with Carlisle winning 2-1. His first league game as Carlisle manager was on April 9, at home to Tranmere, the game resulting in a 2-2 draw.

Right from the outset, he immersed himself totally into all aspects of running the club. He was to claim in later years that he had been preparing himself throughout his playing career for the day when he would move into football management. Now he had the opportunity to put everything he had learnt into practice.

One of the first tasks Shankly set about achieving at Carlisle was to create an atmosphere of pride in the club. He ordered new kit for his players, helped to tidy up the rapidly deteriorating terracing and stand and he even mucked in with the junior players, helping them to brush out the dressing rooms and polish the first team's boots. If a job needed doing, Shankly did it with them. With a new air of optimism about the club, results and attendances began to improve.

One of Shankly's first signings at Carlisle was his former team-mate at Preston, Paddy Waters. The Dublin born wing-half had been struggling to regain his first team place at Preston after injury and Shankly offered him a new start at Carlisle. Initially, Waters was not keen to sign as he revealed in 'The Carlisle United Story':

I took one look at Brunton Park and had one thing on my mind... what time is the first train back to Lancashire? It was just like a big, wooden, rabbit hutch. The facilities were shocking, especially for someone like me who'd been used to Preston's ground.

With Shankly's formidable powers of persuasion to the fore, however, Waters decided to sign and he went on to serve Carlisle with distinction for the next eight years. One of Waters' strongest memories of Shankly at Carlisle was the marvellous atmosphere that he seemed to generate:

There was always a great team spirit at Carlisle and always a competition to keep your place. Shankly always had a strong reserve team wherever he's been and it makes for a very determined side. It was just the same at Carlisle in the early 1950s. The place was really buzzing while Shanks was in charge. He lived for football - football mad.

It is interesting to note that the Shankly tactic of rubbishing the opposition, which was used to such good effect by Shankly during his pre-match pep talks at Liverpool, was employed by him from the outset of his managerial career at Carlisle. Paddy Waters recalled the air of excitement around Brunton Park when the players heard that they had been drawn to play Cup holders Arsenal in the FA Cup during the 1950-51 season. Shankly, however, soon put a stop to the euphoria when he summoned his players together before the following day's training: *'Arsenal, who the hell are they? I've never heard of them!'* he quipped before putting his players through their morning session.

On the day of the match, Shankly sent out his team to play their illustrious opponents at Highbury, determined not to be overawed by either the opposition or the occasion. The ploy worked and Carlisle brought off the shock of the day holding Arsenal to a 0-0 draw. Hopes were high that Carlisle could finish off the job in the replay and the team's confidence was further boosted when Shankly rushed into the dressing room, shut the door and excitedly told them:

Boys, I've just seen them getting out of their coach. They should be in hospital. They're in a right state. The centre-forward can hardly walk.

Similar to many a Liverpool team a decade later, the Carlisle players ran out onto the pitch thinking they were about to take on a bunch of half fit has-beens. In the early part of the game, the Shankly tactic worked with Carlisle more than holding their own. The turning point of the game, however, was when a strong challenge from one of the tough tackling Arsenal defenders effectively put Carlisle's danger man, winger Billy Hogan, out of the match. After this incident, Arsenal's class began to tell and, in the end, they ran out comfortable 4-1 winners.

It was at Carlisle that he first began to harness the Shankly masterplan of the fans and the club being one. When an opposition eleven stepped out to play a Shankly team, they weren't taking on eleven players but the club as a whole. Within a short space of time, Shankly became a firm favourite with the Carlisle supporters. Before every home game, he would speak to them over the tannoy, explaining the reasons behind any team changes and giving summaries of how the club had been playing in away matches. As was the case with practically every player who was fortunate to have him as a manager, the Carlisle players, particularly the younger ones, were totally bowled over by the infectious enthusiasm of their new manager. Average players were made to feel like internationals; to the young players he was something of a father figure.

In his autobiography, Shankly spoke of the style of management he set out to achieve and described how he hoped to treat his players:

I was determined to be fair with them, instead of victimising them, punishing them, fining them, castigating them or humiliating them at the wrong time or in front of the wrong people. I would not have favourites. A player could be my biggest enemy but if he could play I would say he was great. If he didn't like me, it didn't make any difference to my judgement. Throughout my time at Preston I saw favouritism. 'Jimmy is a nice little chap' they said, so Jimmy would play even though he wasn't as good a player as Peter. I saw that happening and I saw it was wrong.

Throughout his managerial career, Shankly stuck to the man-management blueprint that he devised at Carlisle and it was a plan that would be a crucial element in the creation of his great Liverpool teams.

After two happy seasons at Brunton Park, during which he took them to the brink of promotion to Division Two, Shankly applied for the vacant manager's job at Grimsby Town. Lack of finance to back the ambitious Shankly was always going to be a problem at Carlisle but Grimsby, who had recently been relegated to the Third Division, impressed Shankly as a club with First Division potential. Shankly had, in fact, first been approached by Grimsby in the spring of 1951, when he was offered the coach's position at Blundell Park. Carlisle, keen to hold on to the man who was breathing new life into the club, increased his salary to ward off the Grimsby advances. When Charles Spencer resigned as the Grimsby manager at the end of the 1950-51 season, however, the Grimsby board knew the man they wanted and were delighted when Shankly accepted their offer.

Although both the club and its supporters, many of whom remembered losing Shankly as a player to Preston in 1933, were deeply unhappy at his decision to leave Carlisle, it was with their good wishes that he left Brunton Park and the club that launched him into professional football as both a player and a manager. The vacant manager's post at Carlisle was taken by Fred Emery but Shankly was obviously a hard act to follow as former international footballer and later renowned sports journalist, Ivor Broadis, once remarked:

Following Bill Shankly at Carlisle with his match day talk to the fans over the loud speaker system must have been like following Sammy Davis at the London Palladium.

When Shankly arrived at Grimsby, the squad of players he had to work with was somewhat depleted after the sale of some of the club's better players.

Shankly with his Grimsby Town team, 1953.

After making some astute moves into the transfer market, Shankly quickly built a talented team of players who had proven league experience. He quickly had them playing as a unit and the team narrowly missed out on promotion to Division Two in his first season at the club.

Employing the same type of training methods that he had begun at Carlisle, with the emphasis on ball-work, team-work and set-piece plays, the Grimsby team once again pushed hard for promotion during the 1952-53 season but fell away towards the end of the campaign, finishing fifth in the League.

With the Grimsby team in need of an injection of new players and not a great deal of money available to bring them to Blundell Park, Shankly felt he was not in a position to improve the Humberside club's prospects and took up an offer from Workington to help them avoid losing their Football League status. After guiding Tranmere Rovers during the 1953 Christmas and Boxing Day games, Shankly resigned as Grimsby manager and took over at Workington on January 6, 1954. An added incentive to Shankly was the promise of a bonus payment if he saved the club from going out of the League.

When Shankly arrived at the Third Division (North) club, they were in a desperate position. Their previous manager, Ted Smith, had left football to

28

take up the offer of employment in the prison service and the managerless team were lying at the bottom of the division. Tommy Jones, who was club coach at Workington, was doing his best to get the club away from the foot of the table but it was clear that strong managerial direction was needed to help stem the tide of poor results. With the arrival of Shankly and the boost of new players at the club, most of whom were signed by the Workington board before Shankly's arrival, the team began to show an improvement in form and finished the season a couple of places clear of the dreaded re-election zone.

A couple of items of information about Workington that Shankly had not been informed of at his interview for the job were that the club still had gas lighting and Workington Rugby League team also trained and played their home games on the same Borough Park pitch that the football team played on. The churning up of the pitch by the rugby team did not go down at all well with Shankly!

As was the case with every club he was involved with, Shankly became involved with all aspects of running the club at Workington. A great deal of his free time was spent fund-raising or organising Sunday morning training sessions for the youth team.

What Shankly had not yet developed was his rapport with the press and media that was so marked during the Liverpool years. When members of the local press arrived at the ground to try to get an interview with the Workington boss, they would be sent away empty handed after being informed that he was involved in a tactical talk with the team, or he was out on his daily jog. Likewise, if they called at his house, he would either be in the bath or out training.

Shankly spent the summer months at Workington restructuring his playing staff and set out to build a team who would be capable of putting in a challenge for promotion to Division Two. Similar to the methods he brought in at his two previous clubs, Shankly introduced new training methods which were designed not only to get the players super fit but also to build up team spirit. Players who played under Shankly at Workington were amazed at how quickly Shankly was able to get them to regard training as an enjoyable experience rather than a chore. He even introduced an end of training five-a-side, which was always the married men against the bachelors, with Shankly captain of the married men. From all accounts the ribbing between the teams helped to create a bond of comradeship that pulled the players together.

Inspired by the Shankly magic, Workington began the 1954-55 season with a flourish and at the beginning of December were just four points off the top spot in the League. The team was playing good, entertaining football and the general atmosphere at Borough Park was one of optimism. The second round of the FA Cup also brought a result and a chance meeting that delighted and inspired Shankly and his Workington players.

Workington were drawn away to Leyton Orient, who were doing well near the top of the division (South). Shankly and his team set off the evening before the match to catch the midday Flying Scotsman to London. Once settled on the train Shankly got word that the legendary Hungarian team of Puskas, Koesis and company were also on the train, travelling back to London after defeating Shankly's beloved Scotland 4-2 at Hampden Park. Shankly lost no time in telling his players to follow him and to make the acquaintance of a team that were widely regarded as the greatest team in the world. The Hungarians were only too happy to exchange pleasantries with the Workington team and both sets of players conversed, as best they could, for the remainder of the journey. Shankly, in fact, obtained the signatures of the Hungarian team on a postcard and it was a memento of the occasion that he would always treasure. On reaching London, the two teams said their goodbyes and Workington set off to take on Leyton Orient. Workington, obviously drawing inspiration from their chance meeting with the Hungarian legends, won with a goal from Bertolini.

The celebrations at Borough Park were complete when a postcard arrived from the Hungarian FA congratulating Workington on their *'historic win over Leyton Orient.'*

Workington's cup run came to an end in the next round when Luton overwhelmed them 5-0. Their league form also became inconsistent but they still managed to finish a creditable eighth. Before the season was over, Shankly began to prepare for the following season's campaign. Always on the lookout for young talent, he placed an advert in the local press advising all young footballers in the county to write to him and he would fix them up with a trial. In fact, his youth policy blossomed to such an extent that the reserve team were now known as the 'Shankly Babes' and were drawing crowds of 2,000 plus at home games.

The start of the 1955-56 season saw Workington once again riding high near the top of the League and expectations were high that the team would be able to sustain their promotion challenge during this campaign. The beginning of November saw them defeating Barrow 6-1 but, a week later, the club was brought down to earth with a 5-1 defeat at Accrington Stanley, followed a few days later by the body blow of Shankly deciding to take up the offer of the assistant manager's post at Huddersfield Town. The offer had been put to Shankly by his former Preston team-mate, Andy Beattie, who was manager at Huddersfield.

Shankly, who had no contract at Workington, had found managing the West Cumberland team a hard but enjoyable experience. The club was being run on a shoestring and had to depend on donations from its Auxiliary Association, Supporter's Club and other fund-raising activities for its survival.

The boardroom wrangling at Workington was always a source of amusement to Shankly and he once commented that to witness the arguments and resignations that seemed to take place every week was *better than going to the pictures.* Even after his departure from Borough Park, Shankly kept in touch with goings-on at the club through correspondence with club groundsman, Billy Watson. Shankly would often enquire after the board members and would give them nicknames similar to the names of American gangsters from the prohibition era. One board member, Jack Wannop, was always referred to as Johnny Bunny, one of Al Capone's notorious henchmen.

The impact that Shankly had on Workington and the players who were members of Shankly's team at Borough Park can be gauged from a series of interviews with former Workington players who played under him, conducted by Martin Wingfield for his book 'So Sad, So Very Sad... The League History of Workington AFC' (1992). Ted Cushin recalled:

He had the ability to make his players feel ten feet tall. He never shouted at a player, indeed rarely raised his voice at all - except to blame the referee!

Rex Dunlop is another former Workington player on whom Shankly made a deep impression:

He was a tremendous motivator and had a great sense of humour. On one occasion after beating high-flying Barnsley 2-0 at Borough Park he turned and said 'I wish to hell we would play like them!'

Jack Vitty, who was appointed team captain by Shankly recalled:

A local firm, the Tognarelli family, who specialized in ice-cream production, gave an 'Ice-cream Ball' for the Workington players and wives at the Central Hotel, where Shankly was staying having just taken up the post of Workington manager. Shanks displayed his well-known aversion to anything not connected to football by keeping guard in the hotel foyer until the end of the function, instead of retiring to bed at 10.30 as usual. The players all felt that 'Big Brother' was watching them - but he failed to detect the odd drink hidden behind potted palms!

One Workington player who did fall foul of Shankly's no alcohol policy, however, was Ernie Whittle. Whittle, a player whose skill and goal scoring ability were regarded by Shankly as one of the main reasons for Workington avoiding the drop out of the Football League, had a few too many after one game and news of Ernie's breaching the Shankly code of conduct reached his teetotal boss. Whittle was summoned into Shankly's office and was fined a week's wages. Later in the day, however, Shankly discovered that Whittle, who was one of only a small number of English players with the Cumbrian club, had recently been on the receiving end of what was intended as good natured ribbing from the Scottish contingent at the club. To Ernie it was all getting rather tiresome and he had decided to drown his sorrows with a few pints. With this in mind, Shankly decided to pay Whittle a visit. He then told a bewildered Whittle to get into the car with him and proceeded to drive the player to the nearest shopping centre. Still not knowing the purpose of his unexpected visit to town, Whittle was taken by Shankly to a local tailors shop, where a new suit was purchased for him by his idiosyncratic manager. It is highly likely that the cost of the new suit was probably greater than the week's wages that Shankly had fined the player but to Shankly it was probably his way of showing a player he held in high regard, that he knew what he was going through and that he was not on his own. To this day it is a gesture that Whittle has not forgotten.

Billy Watson, the Workington groundsman with whom Shankly struck up an immediate friendship, recalled the afternoon tea breaks in the boiler room with Shankly:

I can still hear his steel-tipped heels as he walked down the tunnel. He would pull up a lemonade crate to sit on and I would say to myself in anticipation, 'What will he reminisce about today?' Would it be his own Tom Finney, or maybe West Brom's Ronnie Starling with his emerald green overcoat. Maybe it would be that autographed postcard from the world-beating Hungarian team he met on the train when the Reds went to Leyton Orient and defeated them in the FA Cup. He treasured that. His marvellous laugh as he tells me yet again about the old lady in Cleaton Moor trying to hit him with her walking stick and shouting 'Get back to Workington!' Because his 'A' team had just beaten her beloved Cleaton Moor Celtic. You can't buy memories like that.

Although unhappy to see him leave, the Workington board wished Shankly well and, according to all accounts, it was an amicable parting. A fact borne out 25 years later, when he returned to Borough Park, in August 1980, to open the 'Shankly Lounge'.

Shankly's task at Huddersfield was to help Andy Beattie pull the club away from the foot of Division One. He was also given the task of developing the club's youth policy. Despite the presence of Shankly, Huddersfield failed to avoid relegation to Division Two at the end of the 1955-56 season.

The start of the new season saw Shankly still in charge of the reserve team and among the fine crop of youngsters that were being groomed by Shankly for the first team were future England internationals, Ray Wilson and Mike O'Grady, plus a fifteen year old Scot who, with Wilson, would develop into one of the game's greats: Dennis Law.

Law was already on Huddersfield's books when Shankly arrived at the club but had yet to sign professional terms. It was obvious to Shankly from his first look at Law in action that the club had an incredible player on their hands but the Scottish youth was so frail - weighing less than seven stone - that Shankly put him on a steak and milk diet in an attempt to build him up. Recalling his first sight of Dennis Law, Shankly later wrote in his autobiography:

Right from the start Dennis stood out with his enthusiasm and will to win - nastiness, if you like. He would have died to have won. He had a temper, and was a terror - a bloody terror, with ability.

Shankly was also grooming future England international, Ray Wilson, during this period and was responsible for Wilson's conversion from a wing-half into a full-back. Interviewed by Ken Rogers for his book 'Everton Greats' (1989), Wilson recalled his former manager at Huddersfield:

I remember Bill Shankly's five-a-side games at Huddersfield. He would keep four Scots to make up his side against five Englishmen. It was England v Scotland on the asphalt car park at Leeds Road under the mill and the gasometer. We would keep playing until Scotland got in front and that was that!

Despite the image that Shankly would often project as the tough Scot who stood no nonsense, Wilson remembers Shankly differently:

People talk about Shankly being a hard man. In my experience he found it difficult to come down on people. He played the role of his favourite film star, James Cagney, the little tough guy. Deep down he was not a tough individual himself. It was just enthusiasm with Bill, almost a boyish approach to the game he loved.

Dennis Law, remembering Shankly from this period, recalled that Shankly would always fill him with confidence and make him feel cocky. *'Forget your strengths, work on your weaknesses'* he would constantly tell him.

During the early part of the 1956-57 season, Shankly's reserve team were going well and some of the Shankly youngsters were pushing for first team places. In contrast, the Huddersfield first team had made an unconvincing start to the campaign and, after three successive defeats, Andy Beattie resigned the manager's position and Shankly took over on November 5, 1956.

Although Shankly was happy now to be in charge of a club of Huddersfield Town's calibre, taking over from his friend Andy Beattie was always a source of embarrassment to him. The ideal situation to him would have been a partnership but it was not to be and, although uneasy about taking the place of his great pal at the helm of Huddersfield, it did not hinder their friendship, which lasted throughout Shankly's Liverpool years.

With Shankly now in charge, initial results were promising but a four match losing run leading up to the Christmas fixtures revealed to Shankly that regaining their First Division status was not going to be easy. Shankly had by now introduced several of his teenage prodigies into the first team and was delighted to see Dennis Law score his first league goal for the club against Notts County on Boxing Day, 1956. Shankly was also pleased to see a man who will always be a folk hero on Merseyside, Dave Hickson, hitting the net regularly for Town. However, the season ended in disappointment for Huddersfield, who could only finish in mid-table.

Ray Wilson remembers a game during his time playing for Huddersfield when Charlton were leading 4-0 at half-time, with Huddersfield pinned in their penalty area for most of the first 45 minutes. As the despondent team sat in the dresing room, Shankly applied his famous psychology:

Four breakaways, that's all they've had. Now in the second half you'll murder them!

The following season saw Shankly and Huddersfield involved in two major fights: one to gain promotion, the other to hang on to Dennis Law. Law was by now seventeen and had yet to sign as a professional with the club. Most of the top clubs in Britain were now on the trail of the teenage sensation and it looked likely that Huddersfield would lose him. It was only after much persuasion by Shankly that Dennis Law finally decided to sign himself to Huddersfield Town. As players who joined Liverpool in later years would

confirm, when Shankly was in full flow, he was an expert at coaxing players to sign on the dotted line.

Even with Law in the team, Huddersfield failed to maintain a promotion push and finished a disappointing ninth in the League. It was obvious that, despite the fact that Huddersfield was a team sprinkled with fine young players, money was needed to buy that extra class to turn them into a promotion winning team. All through his managerial career, Shankly knew it was no good having ambition without ammunition. He had enormous self belief that he would eventually produce a trophy winning team but he needed a board with the will and the finances to back him.

The club that would do just that, Liverpool, were about to give him the call. The beginning of the 1959-60 season saw Huddersfield make a bright start with five wins out of their first season games. They then went through an inconsistent spell and it was obvious to Shankly that, unless the club allowed him to strengthen the team, promotion would not be forthcoming.

Shankly watches as 17-year-old Dennis Law signs on the dotted line for Huddersfield, 1957.

After a poor home performance against Cardiff City, which saw them lose 1-0, he was approached by Liverpool Chairman, Tom Williams, and a director, Harry Latham. After exchanging pleasantries, they asked Shankly if he would be interested in taking over the best team in the country. Shankly replied: '*I didn't know Matt Busby had retired from Manchester United!*' Nevertheless, Shankly was interested, for he knew of the untapped potential that existed at Anfield. Liverpool was a big city club just waiting for a messiah to transform it from a slumbering giant into a football institution. Shankly was later to claim that it was his destiny to go to Liverpool.

Although Shankly did not relish the thought of having to leave behind the youngsters he had been grooming to stardom, such as Law and Wilson, the temptation to join Liverpool was too strong and after his last game in charge of Huddersfield, ironically against Liverpool on November 28, 1959, Shankly decided to accept Liverpool's offer.

If Shankly's decision was probably the most significant in the history of Liverpool Football Club, it turned out to be a catastrophic one for Huddersfield Town. It may be conjecture but it seems highly likely that if finance had been made available to Shankly, and taking into consideration the talented youngsters that Huddersfield had at their disposal, the incredible success that Liverpool were to achieve under Shankly could surely have been, at the very least, partly emulated by the Yorkshire club.

Perhaps the potential was not there for Shankly to mould and harness the Huddersfield Town supporters into the 'Red Army' at Anfield that was so crucial to Liverpool's success but it is possible that Town, with Shankly at the helm, could have at least enjoyed the same level of success that their Yorkshire rivals, Leeds United, achieved in the 1960s and 70s. On leaving Hudddersfield to become Liverpool's manager, he told his players: '*I'm going to a place where they live, eat, sleep and drink football. And that's my place.*'

King Of The Kop

HUDDERSFIELD'S loss was Liverpool's gain and, on December 14, 1959, Shankly officially took over as manager and set about turning Liverpool into the best club in Britain.

Within a short time Shankly soon realised that both the team and ground were not adequate for Liverpool Football Club. The back room staff were no problem; Shankly regarded them as a team of assistants he could work with. He demanded loyalty and told them he would not tolerate any back-biting. In return, he promised them the same loyalty and respect. As the success of later years would show, the team of Paisley, Bennett and Fagan, led by manager Shankly, would develop into a formidable outfit. Bob Paisley recalled:

When Bill came to Liverpool from Huddersfield, a friend at Huddersfield told me I'd never be able to work with Bill for more than two years. I wouldn't be able to stand the strain, he said. But from the moment he arrived we got on like a house on fire. Bill was happy with us and we were certainly happy with him. He carried us along through the sheer force of his personality.

From the outset, Shankly took sole control of team selection and would not tolerate boardroom interference. As was the case with his previous clubs, he immersed himself totally into all aspects of running the club and team preparation. A story that illustrates Shankly's fanatical approach to detail was recently told by popular BBC Radio Merseyside personality, Alan Jackson.

Alan Jackson worked at Anfield during the 1960s, playing pre-match music and making announcements before and during the game. He once received a visit from Shankly in his broadcasting box, who told him: *'Listen son, if you've got to make an announcement during a game, will you please do it when the ball is not in the penalty area.'* The box that Alan sat in did not give him a view of the game, so he had to take a friend along to give him a signal when the ball was well away from the penalty area. With the Liverpool team of this period prone to putting the opposition under constant pressure, Alan had a difficult task trying to fit in his announcements.

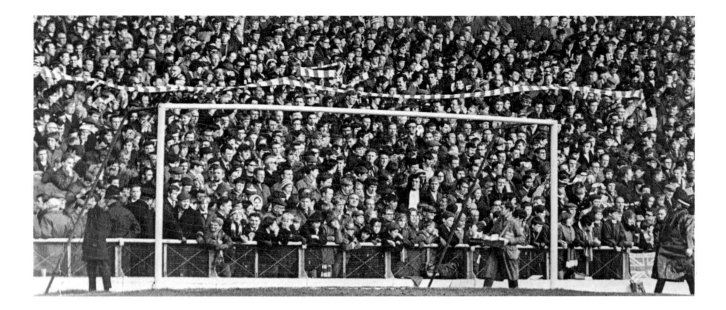

Above: The Kop, early 1960s.

Below: Anfield, 1950s.

Shankly's first game in charge saw Liverpool lose 4-0 to Cardiff City; the task in front of him had been made perfectly obvious. He knew that new blood was needed but the finance to bring new players of the standard Shankly required had not yet been made available to him. An offer was made to Leeds to sign Jack Charlton but the Liverpool board would not meet Leeds' asking price. Shankly then moved in for Scottish international Dave MacKay from Hearts, but lost out when Spurs put in a higher bid and snatched the tough tackling half-back from under Liverpool's nose. If Liverpool were to compare with the best, then Shankly would need a key figure on the board who shared the same visions and aspirations for the club as he did and would back up these ambitions with hard cash.

At his previous club, Huddersfield, Shankly was confident that if the money had been made available to him to purchase a couple of key players, then he could have built them into a First Division team. Ray Wilson, recalling his Huddersfield days once said:

You felt Shankly was the only manager in the world who might spend his own money to buy players.

Shankly was clearly disgruntled about the lack of finance available to him during his early days at Liverpool and on several occasions came close to quitting the managership. Sir Matt Busby in his book 'Soccer at the Top' (1973) recalled one such occasion:

Somebody at Liverpool had rubbed him up the wrong way, so much that he told me that he was going to resign. I asked him if he had a job to go to and he hadn't. Bill Shankly was always so infatuated with football that money was coincidental to the job and the game. Whatever the trouble was, he felt it strongly, and the fact that he would not have a job and therefore would not have any wages would scarcely have entered his head. There was something he didn't like and he would go. It was as simple as that. I influenced him to stay. I said: 'Bill, things are bound to break for you.' In only a few weeks after that they did begin to break for him and Liverpool became a power in the land.

Shankly was desperate for money to be made available to him at Liverpool and to his relief a soul mate arrived on the board in the shape of Eric Sawyer. Sawyer was a key figure in the Littlewoods Pools organisation and was obviously aware of what a cash injection could achieve at the club after witnessing the rejuvenation of Everton after being given financial backing from Littlewoods founding figure, John Moores, who had joined the Everton board in the late 1950s.

Sawyer was confident that if Shankly was given the same financial assistance, Merseyside would soon have two teams challenging for the game's top honours. Once given the green light, Shankly knew the players he wanted and moved quickly to bring Ron Yeats and Ian St John, the backbone of Liverpool's success in the 1960s, to Anfield. He lost no time in appointing the massive Yeats as team captain telling the player he called his 'Red Colossus': *You're so big that when you lead the team out you'll frighten people!'*

With the two Scots supplementing Hunt and a squad of players that included Leishman, Moran, Melia, Byrne and Milne, Shankly was now confident that he had a team that was capable of achieving not only promotion to the First Division but could more than hold their own at the highest level.

After the disappointment of missing promotion in the 1960-61 campaign, finishing in third spot behind champions Ipswich and runners-up Sheffield United, they finally clinched a place back in the top flight with a 2-0 home win against Southampton. It had taken a couple of seasons to achieve but the Liverpool bandwagon was now finally on the rails.

It was during this promotion winning season that the amazing Shankly relationship with the Anfield regulars and, in particular, the Kop, began to manifest itself. Liverpool had always been a city that prided itself on its wit and self expression but simultaneous with the Merseybeat explosion, led by the Beatles, came the rise of its two football teams. It was this football success, coupled with the Merseybeat music that was enchanting the world, that encouraged the Goodison and Anfield regulars to give full vent to their cocky chanting, singing and merciless taunting of the opposition.

Right from the outset of his managerial career, it was Shankly's aim to harness both the team and the supporters into one. To him, football was a communal experience: the team was an extension of the fans on the pitch and the fans an extension of the team on the terraces. As the Liverpool team paraded around Anfield after clinching promotion to the sound of the Kop chanting in unison, 'Liv-er-pool', Shankly knew he had achieved his objective of building a Liverpool team that, at Anfield at least, was the size of an army.

Interviewed in the mid 1960s, Shankly spoke of his admiration for the Anfield faithful:

The word 'fantastic' has been used many times, but I think there must be another word to describe the Anfield spectators. I think it's more than a fanaticism. It's a religion with them. The thousands who come here to worship...

It's a sort of shrine - it isn't a football ground. These people are not simply fans, they are more like members of a tremendous family.

Another Merseyside football legend, Joe Mercer, was once asked about Shankly's relationship with the Liverpool supporters:

From the moment he arrived there's been only one way - up. And this endless success was mirrored in that amazing relationship with the Kop. When he was at Anfield he was the city of Liverpool's answer to vandalism and hooliganism, because the kids came to see Liverpool. They came to see those red shirts and Shankly was their man, their hero, their football god. He belongs to the Kop - he's one of them. If he hadn't managed Liverpool I'm sure he'd have been on the Kop dressed in red, singing and chanting 'Liverpool, Liverpool'.

Shankly's First Great Team

LIVERPOOL began the 1962-63 season in an unconvincing way. Shankly put this down to giving too much respect to the opposition and he wasted no time in correcting his Liverpool team's psychological approach to playing First Division opposition. He rubbished the opposition mercilessly. Tottenham Hotspur became 'The Drury Lane Fan Dancers'. The team that could boast such outstanding players as Greaves and MacKay were labelled by Shankly as 'a bunch of soft southerners'. West Ham and all the London clubs were given the same treatment. He would watch them getting off the coach and then report to his team: *'They won't last ten minutes against us. Let's hit 'em for five and teach them a lesson.'*

Sometimes his team would gather round a small table containing Subbuteo players representing Liverpool's opponents. One by one, he would pluck the miniature figures from the table putting them in his coat pocket as he vilified each member of the team: *'Goalkeeper, too old; full-backs, past it; centre-half, overrated.'* If there were a couple of figures left on the table, perhaps current internationals who were at the top of their form, he would simply tell his team *'Christ boys, if you can't beat a bunch of has-beens and a couple of decent players, you don't deserve to be representing Liverpool!'*

In later years some of the best teams on the continent were also given the same treatment, with Ajax labelled 'a bunch of peasants' and Red Star Belgrade 'a load of pansies' - typical Shankly sentiments about two of Europe's best teams. Obviously he didn't believe his analysis of the opposition, neither did his team but somehow it worked; the Liverpool players would run out on to the pitch with their confidence sky high.

Gradually results improved and Liverpool made progress up the table to finish eighth. Hopes were high at Anfield that this may be the year that they would finally break their FA Cup duck but an unlucky 1-0 defeat to a Gordon Banks-inspired Leicester City in the semi-final put paid to any Wembley dreams for another year. The season finished, in fact, with city rivals, Everton, being crowned league champions. Shankly, never one to give credit to 'that lot across the park' claimed that Leicester City was undoubtedly the best team in the League.

The following season 1963-64 was to prove a momentous one for Liverpool with the First Division championship making the short journey across Stanley Park to the trophy cabinet at Anfield. The season actually started badly for the team, with an away victory at Blackburn followed by two home defeats. Shankly held a post-mortem and asked every one of the players for their views and ideas. Ron Yeats told the Liverpool Echo: *'With Bill Shankly it's not just a question of him telling you. He wants you to tell him.'*

Shankly's heart-to-heart with his team revealed that they were ever anxious to perform well in front of their own supporters and Shankly, a master at preparing his team psychologically, soon had his players performing at Anfield in a more relaxed frame of mind. Within no time, they were back to winning ways and, inspired by new signing Peter Thompson and the probing midfield play of Willie Stevenson, who had been signed the previous season but was now beginning to display the form Shankly knew he was capable of, Liverpool now looked a polished team.

Shankly had promised the Liverpool shareholders at the end of the 1962-63 campaign that the league championship would be theirs next season and with Roger Hunt scoring thirty-one league goals in front of an Anfield average attendance of 50,000, Liverpool stormed to the title. By now, the Kop had taken to singing Beatles' songs, often changing the words slightly to pay homage to their heroes with 'We love you yeah, yeah, yeah' becoming a particular favourite.

The key to much of Liverpool's success that season was the probing wing play of Callaghan and Thompson and even Everton legend Dixie Dean was so impressed by the Liverpool wing pair's standard of play that he told a daily paper: *'If I'd have played with those two feeding me the crosses, I'd have scored 100 league goals, never mind 60!'*

Although they won the title with some ease, the FA Cup once again eluded Liverpool. After reaching the quarter-finals, the team were drawn against Swansea Town. Hopes were high that Liverpool would contest the semi-finals for the second year on the run, for Swansea were hovering near the foot of Division Two and victory for Liverpool looked a formality. The magic of the FA Cup, however, threw up another freak result and Swansea, inspired by an outstanding performance by international goalkeeper, Noel Dwyer, defied wave after wave of Liverpool attacks to win 2-1. After the game, a disgruntled Shankly told an incredulous press that his team should have won 14-0. A Swansea official, overhearing the remark, quickly corrected him stating: *'Sorry Bill, it should have been 14-2!'*

A growing feature of Liverpool's play during their championship winning year was their outstanding fitness and stamina. One of the team, Roger Hunt, recalled in his autobiography:

Bill Shankly always claimed Liverpool was the fittest team in the country and he was right. In game after game we took control because even if our opponents could match us for skill, they could not match us at producing it right at the end. Invariably they ran out of steam in the second half, whereas we managed to keep on going.

Apart from their superb physical fitness, another key reason for Liverpool's success during this period was the fact that they were a team that was always alert to danger - even when the ball was out of play. With this aspect of Liverpool's play in mind, Shankly once remarked: *'When the ball's dead, Liverpool come alive.'* Liverpool clinched the title during the 1963-64 season with a 5-0 home victory over Arsenal.

With the championship safely in the bag, Liverpool were still left with three games to play. Ron Yeats, the Liverpool captain, recalled in a Radio City interview that Shankly wanted to finish the season with a certain amount of panache:

I remember he said to Tommy Lawrence after we had just won the League but still had a few games to play out the season. 'Tom, wouldn't it be great if we could put a deck chair in the middle of the goal, you sitting in it, cigar in your mouth, and when the ball comes, you get out of your deck chair and catch it and say "It's a lovely day to play football, isn't it?".'

Towards the end of the 1963-64 season an event took place at Goodison Park which displayed the growing esteem that Shankly was being held in, not just by the Liverpool players but others who came into contact with him. A benefit game was arranged at Goodison for former Everton legend, 'Dixie' Dean. The Scottish players of Everton and Liverpool were to play the English of the two teams. The England team was managed by Harry Catterick and Scotland by Shankly.

Interviewed by Ken Rogers, Alec Young revealed that throughout his career at Everton no one ever gave him a pre-match pep talk the way that Shankly did that spring evening:

He made me feel great before the game. I never got that from Harry Catterick or the Everton coaches. It was the only time I was inspired off the park at Goodison. Shankly would always praise his own team and he would have a go at the opposition when it was called for. I really admired Shankly. I think lots of Evertonians did without saying so at the time. It was a great experience having him in the dressing room before the Dean game.

Catterick may have lacked the charisma and motivational abilities of Shankly, but one man on Merseyside who had nothing but admiration for the Everton manager was Shankly himself, and in his autobiography he wrote:

His record speaks for itself and the combination of Harry Catterick and John Moores, a director who knows the game from A to Z, was formidable.

With a tilt at the European Cup to look forward to, Liverpool players reported back for pre-season training for the 1964-65 season in high spirits. As with everything that took place at Anfield, Shankly's preparation for a new season was meticulous. He even decided to change the Liverpool playing strip to all red, explaining: *'It will make the team look even tougher, bigger and more formidable to the opposition.'* It was another typical piece of psychological trickery by Shankly. When the players reported back to Melwood, there would be a gradual build up which was designed to bring the players to a good level of fitness while reducing the risk of pulled muscles; the players would then step up training to get the squad fully fit. Practice matches would take place on a full-size pitch and, after a few days, the practice games would be played on a half-size pitch. Eventually, as top fitness was achieved, the players would play five-a-side games in the penalty area to sharpen up their first touch and distribution, with the confined space leaving little time for dwelling on the ball.

Tommy Smith speaking about Liverpool's training and tactics in 'The Great Derbies' (1988) claimed:

All the time I was at Anfield we never practised a corner or a free kick. The only thing I was ever taught was push-ups; as soon as the opposition got the ball, you push up on a man, not man-to-man marking, just pick up the one nearest, get closer to him so you make it harder for him to find somebody with the ball. I was always taught that if the side is all pulling together, they will cover for a player having a bad time.

The idea for the famous 'sweat box', which was a set of boards placed fifteen yards apart, which a player would go into and then have to blast the ball from board to board for as long as possible, came to Shankly after observing Tom Finney participating in a similar exercise at the back of the Preston North End stand.

Inspecting the pitch before the
European Cup game against
Cologne, 1965.

With a superbly fit squad, coupled with the wonderful camaraderie that Shankly developed at the club, with no room for prima donnas, it was small wonder that the Liverpool team of this period looked capable of brushing aside all before them, including the best that Europe could offer. Evidence that the Liverpool teams of the mid-1960s were a unit, in which the whole was definitely greater than the sum of its parts, can be gauged from the fact that so many of the outstanding Liverpool players would often fail to produce their best form when selected for British international teams. Speaking in the 1970s, Shankly acknowledged that the mid-1960s team at full strength and in reasonable conditions was invincible, *'The best team seen in Britain since the war without a doubt'* was his acclamation of the Ron Yeats led team.

The annual curtain opener to the season, the Charity Shield, saw Liverpool taking on West Ham at Anfield. During the game, Shankly once again showed his affinity for the Liverpool fans, by watching part of the game on his beloved Kop. He sought the supporters' views on the coming season, what they thought of the team and so on. There is little doubt that these views would be entered into the detailed notebook that Shankly always kept throughout his career. It is small wonder that once news of this type of Shankly gesture spread to the Liverpool fans at large, his status as a messiah, who was also one of them, was confirmed. *'Although I'm a Scot, I'd be proud to be called a Scouser'* he once proclaimed and he meant it!

As is usually the case with defending champions, Liverpool struggled to get their momentum going at the start of the 1964-65 season. By the New Year, however, the team looked set for better things in the second half of the season and they were still in Europe having defeated Reykjavik and Anderlecht in the opening two rounds of the European Cup.

After narrowly beating West Brom and Stockport, FA Cup dreams were also still intact. A 1-0 win in the fifth round of the FA Cup against Bolton at Burden Park saw Liverpool in good heart for the European Cup quarter-final tie against Cologne. After two gruelling encounters failed to decide a winner, Liverpool travelled to Rotterdam for a third meeting with the German champions. Even after extra time, the two teams could not be separated and it was only after tossing a disc, which Yeats called correctly, that Liverpool scraped through to face Inter Milan in the semi-finals.

Liverpool's early excursions into Europe were to provide not only memorable matches but also, on occasion, examples of Shankly's humour. During one European trip, a group of Liverpool players arrived back at their hotel slightly later than the time Shankly had stipulated. He immediately began to tear a strip off them and then noticed that model professional Ian Callaghan was among them: *'Jesus, is that you Callaghan? I'm surprised at you. That's it, I'm telling your wife of you!'* he told the startled winger, with his team-mates bursting to laugh but not daring to.

In the FA Cup, Liverpool gained revenge on bogey team Leicester City, to line up a semi-final tie with Tommy Docherty's emerging youngsters, Chelsea. The only goal of the game, scored by wing wizard Peter Thompson, saw Liverpool through to their first FA Cup Final since their 1950 defeat at the hands of Arsenal. In the Final, Liverpool were to meet Leeds United, a team involved in some epic matches against Liverpool in the mid-1960s and most of the 1970s.

Liverpool's Wembley appearance in 1965 saw the spontaneous singing and humour of Shankly's Red Army at its peak. At no other ground in Britain was one treated to the wit and sheer exuberance that were a feature of Anfield during this period. No one was spared from their humorous and often barbed chants and songs.

On the morning of the final, even Prime Minister Harold Wilson was given a taste of the Kop choir when he was aroused inside No 10 Downing Street by a group of Liverpool fans outside the famous residence chanting: *'ee-aye-addio, Harold's still in bed'*. Harold in fact had been up for quite a while and went outside to chat to the fans.

During the pre-match build up, Shankly had been kept busy all week, speaking to the media, looking after his team and answering a multitude of requests for Cup Final tickets. Chief scout at Liverpool during this period was Norman Low and he has a story that displays both Shankly's caustic humour and his affection for the Kop:

We were in the office together a few days before the FA Cup Final against Leeds. The phone went, Bill picked it up and I could hear the fellow on the other end. He had a strong Birmingham accent. Bill says 'Yes, yes, what do you want, sir?' The fellow said 'Did you get my letter?' 'What letter? Would it be after tickets?' 'Yes, I wrote to you from Birmingham.' Shankly exploded 'Birmingham, Birmingham, Birmingham? I wouldn't give a drop of my blood to Birmingham! You know what, sir, You know what? I've got a hundred relatives and there's not one of those beggars getting a ticket. They're going to the boys on the Kop, any tickets I've got. By Christ, Birmingham, Birmingham!' 'But Mr Shankly, I was born in Liverpool.' 'Were you, by Christ! Well by the sound of your voice you've been away a bloody long time. You'll get no tickets here!'

On the morning of the match, the Liverpool team relaxed by listening to Shankly on the radio. He was the guest castaway on 'Desert Island Discs'. By all accounts, his selection of records consisted mainly of Kop favourites such as the Beatles and Gerry and the Pacemakers. By the time the team reached the dressing rooms, Shankly had them well prepared. Roger Hunt claimed that Shankly's pre-match pep talk was so good that they walked out onto the Wembley turf convinced that they were going to win.

Goals by St John and Hunt brought the FA Cup back to Anfield for the first time in Liverpool's history but the real Wembley hero was left-back Gerry Byrne. Shankly once said:

For a player to be good enough to play for Liverpool, he must be prepared to run through a brick wall for me and then come out fighting on the other side.

Byrne's performance for Liverpool that day epitomised everything that Shankly wanted in a player. Injured in the first minutes of the game after a heavy tackle from Bobby Collins, Byrne sustained a broken collar-bone. The fact that he continued to play for the rest of the game, plus extra time, without once revealing to the opposition the extent of this injury and the obvious pain he must have been suffering, was one of the most heroic Wembley performances of all time. Substitutes had not yet been introduced, so for a ten man Liverpool to have beaten a strong Leeds team was very improbable. After the game, Shankly paid tribute to Gerry Byrne who, even today, is still troubled by the injury he sustained that day, by suggesting that the full-back should have been given all eleven medals.

Anfield salutes the League Championship winning team of 1963-64.

Within days of the Wembley triumph, Liverpool was due to play the first leg of the European Cup semi-final against Inter Milan. Shankly pulled off a wonderful piece of psychological one-upmanship by sending out the injured Byrne and Gordon Milne, who missed the Cup Final through injury, to parade the FA Cup to the Liverpool fans. This gesture drove the crowd into a frenzy and, by the time the Inter players stepped out onto the pitch, they knew they were staring defeat in the face. Liverpool ran out comfortable 3-1 winners against the European Cup favourites and looked forward to completing the job in the return leg.

If the atmosphere at Anfield had been hysterical, the reception that greeted the Liverpool team as they ran out at the San Siro stadium can only be described as hostile. Church bells had kept them awake on the eve of the match and smoke bombs and klaxon horns kept the team on their toes throughout the game. Dubious refereeing decisions added to Liverpool's woes and it was no surprise to see Inter pull back the deficit and eventually run out 3-0 winners. Shankly's dream of completing a unique FA Cup, European Cup double was over but Shankly had seen nothing in Europe that frightened him. Interviewed in the Liverpool Echo, he declared:

In the European Cup you meet cunning, bluff and gimmicks. Don't get me wrong, I am not one of those people who believe that the world ends at the White Cliffs of Dover. I am all for the Soccer Common Market. My only concern is to halt a naive swing in the opposite direction and the belief that the Latins rule the waves. So much of the continental game is based on the safety first principle, to the detriment of entertainment.

With entertainment in mind, Liverpool set out to regain the First Division title in 1965-66 and by October had recorded some stunning victories, including a 5-1 win at West Ham and a 5-0 trouncing of Everton at Anfield. The victory over Everton was in part due to Shankly's ability to send his team out with an incredible psychological advantage over the opposition. During the run up to the game, Shankly had been dropping hints to Bob Paisley - making sure that his team could overhear his remarks - that he had been watching Everton training from his house near Bellefield, Everton's training ground. Knowing that Paisley enjoyed a flutter, he was told by Shankly to get the best odds he could on a Liverpool victory. He told Paisley:

I've been watching them; Catterick has got them running lap after lap around Bellefield, they'll be knackered by Saturday!

As the Everton players arrived at Anfield on Saturday afternoon, Shankly stood in his usual spot watching the opposition arriving at the ground and

making their way across the dressing room corridors. Shankly rushed back to the Liverpool dressing room hardly able to contain himself. *'They can hardly walk, they look shattered!'* The Liverpool team took it all in and went out to face Everton feeling they were about to take on a team of geriatrics. The ploy worked a treat with Liverpool running Everton ragged as they romped to an easy win. The fact that Shankly would have had to climb on his roof to have spied on Everton never entered his team's mind.

The Kop overflows during the Liverpool v Celtic European Cup Winners' Cup second leg game at Anfield, 1966.

Shankly was also not averse to attempting to gain a psychological advantage away from the confines of Anfield and would always accompany his players if they found themselves up before the FA at disciplinary hearings. The late Ted Croker, who was secretary of the FA at the time, remembered some of the Shankly performances:

If a Liverpool player was appearing before a commission, Bill Shankly would speak so eloquently and convincingly that members of the commission must have felt that the wrong man had been brought before them! I used to enjoy Bill's impassioned orations.

Apart from their domination of the League, Liverpool also made steady progress through the opening rounds of the European Cup Winners' Cup and, after knocking out some of the top teams in Europe, were drawn to meet Celtic in the semi-finals.

The first leg of the Celtic match took place at a packed Parkhead and Shankly looked forward to doing battle with his old pal, Celtic manager Jock Stein. Celtic, realising their best chance of success was to build a commanding lead to take back to Anfield, piled on the pressure but had to be content with a 1-0 victory. Shankly was later to make accusations, tongue-in-cheek, that he was certain that Jock Stein had had the pitch polished to help Celtic's chances.

In the return leg at Anfield, another tense affair saw Liverpool hang on to record a 2-0 win thanks to goals from Tommy Smith and Geoff Strong. The team were in their first ever European Final and would meet the German club, Borussia Dortmund, in Glasgow, at Hampden Park.

It was shortly after the Celtic games that Liverpool gained another league title with a home win over Chelsea before an ecstatic Kop. After the game, Tommy Docherty said he agreed wholeheartedly with Bill Shankly's sentiments that the Liverpool fans were the best in the world. To many Liverpool fans, the outstanding team of 1965-66 were the best in the club's history.

It was during this period that Bobby Charlton first encountered Bill Shankly at close quarters and could not believe the man's fanaticism. Obviously Manchester United had encountered Liverpool on several occasions at Anfield and Old Trafford since Liverpool's return to the top flight but Charlton had yet to become acquainted with Shankly. Charlton recalled arriving at Old Trafford to watch a reserve team game and was just about to get out of his car:

The passenger door opened and in got Shankly. 'Bobby, Bobby! Everton - have you found out what they've done? They've bought this player that can't play! And they still think they can beat Liverpool!' He just went into this tirade about Everton. I've never, ever heard anyone so fanatical about the game.

With the title safely back at Anfield for another season, Liverpool travelled to Glasgow for the European Cup Winners' Cup final. Torrential rain, however, had turned Hampden into a quagmire and with Liverpool unable to play a free flowing game, the match turned into a hard fought slog. Despite continuous pressure, Liverpool could not gain the upper hand and an extra time winner, against the run of play, saw the Germans take the trophy 2-1. A bitterly disappointed Shankly was quoted after the game as saying:

That lot would be hard fought to hold a place in the English First Division and the two goals they scored were flukes!

Despite this setback, 1966 had been another fine year, not just for Liverpool but Merseyside football in general, with Everton completing a Scouse monopoly of the game's major domestic honours with an FA Cup Final victory over Sheffield Wednesday. We have all heard Shankly's famous quote about there being two great teams on Merseyside: *'Liverpool and Liverpool Reserves'*, but after Everton's success he was moved to pay tribute to both Everton and Liverpool supporters when he said: *'These supporters deserve only the best teams and the best football.'* 1966 was a season when they got just that.

As if Merseyside's success on the domestic front was not enough, England's dramatic World Cup victory set the seal on an unforgettable year. Although England's victory vindicated Shankly's claim that there was nothing to fear from the rest of the world, the World Cup in general did not impress him. He told the Liverpool Echo:

England played the continentals at their own game and beat them. It proved to me that if English clubs wanted to play the continentals at their own defensive game we would beat them, Liverpool included. But would English football fans pay to watch that kind of football every week? In general I thought the World Cup was played in a negative sense and England won with negative football. England played a defensive game like the continentals do and very few of their matches were entertaining to watch. Apart from Portugal, Hungary and Brazil, they were all defensive teams and I was not very impressed by it. The great thing for England was that all their players came to peak form at the right time for the final, just like a good club side and that was why they beat West Germany.

With English football on a high after England's success, both Liverpool and Everton stepped out at Anfield for the pre-season opener, the Charity Shield, with high expectations for the new campaign.

Darling of the Kop, Roger Hunt, together with his England team-mates, Ray Wilson, and Everton's new signing, Alan Ball, paraded the World Cup around Anfield. Shankly was confident that Liverpool would retain the Championship but they struggled and could manage only fifth place in the League.

The FA Cup was also a disappointment, with Everton's new hero, Alan Ball, putting them out of the competition in the fifth round, at Goodison, with the only goal of the game. There was no joy in the European Cup either, with the rapidly emerging Dutch masters Ajax, inspired by Johan Cruyff, running out easy 7-3 winners over the two legs. Shankly was particularly stung by this defeat but remained defiant. He told the Liverpool Echo:

It annoys me to read all this criticism of Liverpool because we failed to beat the defensively minded Ajax. I can say straight out that Ajax would never be able to beat us at Anfield. They scored two goals against us because we had to come out and attack them because of their first leg lead. But I say that if we had wanted to play defensively that night, Ajax would not have scored against us. I will only make changes when I can strengthen my team. I have told my players to ignore criticism, the sort of criticism we received from people - not from the real Liverpool supporters mind you!

Despite these setbacks, the Liverpool fans followed their manager's lead and refused to become downcast. The humour of the Kop was also still very much in evidence and they even found time to pay a somewhat sarcastic tribute to one of England's World Cup heroes, Jack Charlton, when he visited Anfield with his Leeds United team. As he stepped out on to the pitch, the Kop greeted him with a harmonious rendition of the following song to the tune of Al Johnson's 'Mami':

Charlton, Charlton, I'd walk a million miles to the end of your neck, Charlton.

No doubt Jack saw the funny side of the Kop's double-edged tribute. Other Kop favourites during this period included a cruel tribute to Everton's Gordon West - a fine goalkeeper who always enjoyed a spot of banter with the Kop. They would serenade the Everton keeper with a rendition - sung to the tune of 'Hey there, Georgie Girl', a big hit for the Seekers in the mid-1960s;

Hey there, Gordon West, you're a bigger fruit than Georgie Best.

Although the Kop was imitated by other club's supporters, few were able to match the inventiveness of the Liverpool fans of the 1960s.

Shankly's Second Great Team

DESPITE his rejection of any criticism of his team, Shankly knew that new, young talent was needed and his capture of Emlyn Hughes from Blackpool in February, 1967, was to be one of the key signings of Shankly's reign at Anfield. The summer months also saw Ray Clemence arrive at Anfield for a fee of £18,000. Both would become English internationals and would be crucial in the development of Shankly's next great team.

With the players such as Lawrence, Stevenson, Yeats, St John, Hunt and Milne still giving their all to Liverpool's cause, Shankly was reluctant to part with players that had served him so well but the demands of Liverpool's incredible run of success, coupled with the obvious loss of speed and strength that hits all footballers, meant that the team needed rebuilding. The decision to replace some of his players caused Shankly a lot of heartache. Bob Paisley once claimed that:

If Bill had one failing, it was the fact that he did not like to upset players that had done so well for him. He was a softie at heart.

Joe Mercer also claimed that the image that had grown around Shankly as the tough guy figure was untrue. He said:

Bill Shankly is a myth in so many ways. They say he's tough, he's hard, he's ruthless. Rubbish, he's got a heart of gold, he loves the game, he loves his fans, he loves his players. He's like an old Collie dog, he doesn't like hurting his sheep. He'll drive them, certainly, but bite them, never.

Inevitably, the great team of the 1960s began to disband and a new one, built around Tommy Smith, Chris Lawler, Ian Callaghan, Peter Thompson and supplemented by some outstanding signings, began to emerge. One man whom Shankly was desperately keen to be part of his rebuilding process was Howard Kendall. However, Preston, with whom Shankly still had strong links, was not over keen on being seen as a Liverpool nursery. They had already sold Gordon Milne, Peter Thompson and David Wilson to Liverpool during the 1960s and the directors decided, rather than risk the wrath of their fans who had taken to chanting 'Stay away Shankly', to allow their prized possession to join Everton instead. Shankly was incensed when he heard that the transfer had gone through without being given a chance to stake his claim.

In the late 1960s and early 70s Liverpool maintained a high standard but could not win the crucial games that would see them adding to the trophy tally. However, they finally tasted success again in 1972-73.

When Shankly signed Emlyn Hughes from Blackpool, he claimed that he was afraid to go back there for ten years in case they ran him in for theft. If the signing of Hughes for £65,000 was regarded by Shankly as theft, then the capture of Kevin Keegan from Scunthorpe for just £35,000 was quite rightly described by the Liverpool manager as 'robbery without violence'. Originally, Shankly had hoped to persuade Everton to part with David Johnson but Harry Catterick was adamant that none of his players would be joining the arch-enemy. Shankly looked elsewhere for the final piece of his Liverpool team for the 1970s and, after strong recommendation from his old Preston team-mate, Andy Beattie, Shankly made one of his most crucial signings as Liverpool's manager. Kevin Keegan signed for Liverpool towards the end of the 1970-71 season and was taken with the squad to experience the 1971 FA Cup Final.

After travelling to London a few days before the match, Shankly took his players to see a show at the London Palladium. John Toshack in his autobiography recalled that the team were taken back-stage to meet Tommy Cooper and that Shankly could not get over the size of the comedian's feet:

Jesus Christ, son, what size shoes are they? I've sailed to Ireland in smaller boats than that!

The start of the 1971-72 season saw Keegan in the first team and within a short time, the famous Keegan/Toshack partnership was beginning to blossom. With Steve Heighway also beginning to strike terror into the First Division defences on a regular basis, Liverpool was emerging once again as a potent force.

The Liverpool defence, marshalled by Hughes and Smith, now had the added bonus of a towering centre-half in the Yeats mould, Larry Lloyd who, along with Alec Lindsay and Ray Clemence, was now an England regular. Chris Lawler was also playing better than ever. Lindsay, signed in 1969, had to bide his time before he made the left-back position his own but the day of his debut was also to provide another Shankly story.

Lindsay was understandably showing signs of nerves as he waited to take the field for his first appearance in the Liverpool first team. Shankly, noticing this, put his arm around the young full-back and gave him some last minute instructions: *'When you get the ball, I want you to beat a couple of men and smash the ball into the net, just the same way you used to at Bury.'* A bemused Lindsay scratched his head and muttered *'But Boss, that wasn't me, it was Bobby Kerr!'* Shankly turned to Bob Paisley and exclaimed *'Christ Bob! We've signed the wrong player!'*

It was also during this period that Liverpool missed out on another future England player who could have been signed for nothing. Future Ipswich and England star, Kevin Beattie, was invited to Anfield for trials while still in his teens. Beattie travelled to Liverpool but, unsure of his way around the city, could not find Anfield. He decided to make his way home again and missed out on what may have been an even more glittering career with Liverpool than his Ipswich one proved to be.

1971-72 turned out to be both an exciting but ultimately disappointing season for Liverpool. An incredible end of season run saw the team fighting to the finish with both Leeds and Derby for the league title. They needed to win their final game to clinch the title and a Toshack goal at Arsenal in the final minute looked to have won them another championship. Unfortunately the jubilant Liverpool players and fans failed to notice that one of the linesmen had his flag raised and, despite their protests, the goal was disallowed.

The following season 1972-73 Shankly produced yet another championship winning team. Following the Shankly philosophy of playing to their strengths, Liverpool soon began to take a strong grip in the League and, by Easter, they had won an eighth title. In his autobiography, Shankly claimed that it was during this season that the staff devised a system of play which minimised the risk of injuries:

The team played in sections of the field, like a relay. We didn't want players running the length of the field, stretching themselves unnecessarily, so our back men played in one area, and then passed on to the midfield men in their area, and so on to the front men. So, whilst there was always room for individuals within our system, the work was shared out.

The individuals within that system, such as Heighway and Keegan, really began to blossom as the season developed, though Heighway did not always find it easy to adjust to what Shankly demanded of his players. Writing in his autobiography, Heighway recalled incurring the wrath of Shankly after failing to carry out his instructions. Shankly was a great believer in helping out your team-mates if they were having a hard time during a match and he once collared the dashing winger after a match during which full-back, Alec

Lindsay, had been given a rough time: *'Steve, son, if your next door neighbour's house caught fire, what would you do?'* A miffed Heighway, fully aware of what Shankly was getting at snapped back: *'If you'd stop asking silly bloody questions, maybe you'd get a sensible answer from me!'* Shankly was taken aback by Heighway's response but knew he had made his point and the matter was closed.

On another occasion, Shankly had Heighway close to tears after severely reprimanding him at half-time for shooting over the bar rather than passing to a team-mate. Heighway, remembering the occasion, recalled:

I upped and told him he was being bloody stupid. I felt so angry I was close to tears and Joe Fagan was quickly in to tell me to take it easy. Oddly enough, Shanks himself didn't mind my having reacted so fiercely. His words had touched me on the raw and I was still shaking with anger as I went out on the pitch for the second half.

On another occasion during the season, John Toshack also had a bust up with Shankly after failing to get selected for the first leg of the UEFA Cup Final against the German side, Borussia Moenchengladbach. As it turned out, the game was abandoned following torrential rain and was set to be played the following evening.

On the morning of the game Toshack, still aggrieved at not being selected, decided to confront Shankly and words were exchanged between the two men. Toshack, after telling his manager what he could do with his team, decided to drive home to Formby to tell his wife that he would probably be looking for a new club soon. Within minutes of arriving at his house, Shankly was on the phone: *'Hello son, are you not in bed yet?' 'No, Boss, I've only just got home.' 'Well get to your bed, there's a good chance you will be playing tonight.'*

Shankly had obviously spotted in the previous night's high play that the German team looked vulnerable to crosses and would probably have picked Toshack anyway. He also now knew that the player was raring to prove himself. As it turned out, Toshack had an outstanding game, leading his team to a 3-0 win and the incident in his office was a closed book as far as Shankly was concerned. Like the majority of players who were at Anfield during the Shankly reign, Toshack's respect and affection for 'Shanks' did not diminish with the passing of time.

Tommy Smith was another player who, on the odd occasion, was not averse to arguing his point with Shankly. *'Shut up Tommy! And go and make a cup of tea for us. The only person you're scaring is yourself.'* Shankly is reputed to have once told the 'Anfield Iron' during a heated argument. On one occasion Shankly informed Smith: *'Son, you think you're a hard man; this...'* pointing to a photograph he had just taken out of his pocket, *'...was a hard man.'* It was a photograph of American gangster Al Capone! The mutual respect that Shankly and Smith had for each other was always too strong for such a small thing as a personal disagreement to come between them and to this day there is no greater champion of the man that Tommy Smith refers to simply as *'a soccer god'.*

No doubt over the years at Anfield, Shankly had other disagreements with his players but it is a measure of the man that he never appeared to bear a grudge against any of his team who had the nerve to stand up to him. The good of the club and its supporters came first, not his or his players' egos.

Within weeks of winning the championship, Liverpool took its three goal lead to Germany to contest the second leg of the UEFA Cup. Borussia fought back

Liverpool parade the League Championship trophy after playing Leicester at Anfield, 1972-73.

well to take the tie to 3-2 but Liverpool held on to win their first European trophy after nearly ten years of trying. Shankly had built a team who would become a dominant force throughout the 1970s.

Season 1973-74 was to be Shankly's last at Liverpool. Hopes were high that the elusive European Cup would finally find itself in the Anfield trophy cabinet. After a scrappy two-leg victory over Jeunesse Esche at Luxembourg, Liverpool were drawn against Red Star Belgrade. The Yugoslavian team's victory over Liverpool, which was even more convincing than the 4-2 aggregate suggests, meant that Shankly would not emulate the achievement of his great friends, Sir Matt Busby and Jock Stein, in bringing the European Cup to Britain.

Although on the domestic scene Liverpool failed to close the gap that Leeds United had built up and finished the season as runners-up, five points behind their Yorkshire rivals, Shankly's farewell gift to his beloved Anfield was to lead his team to an unforgettable Wembley FA Cup Final victory over Newcastle United. After victories over Doncaster, Carlisle, Ipswich, Bristol City and Leicester, another day out at Wembley was guaranteed for Liverpool

A delighted Shankly holds the UEFA Cup, his first European trophy as Liverpool's manager.

and the Red Army. The Newcastle team with the formidable Malcolm MacDonald leading their attack was expected to provide stern opposition. As it turned out with the rapidly maturing Phil Thompson keeping a firm grip on MacDonald and the rest of the Liverpool team playing at the peak of their form, Liverpool coasted to an easy 3-0 victory.

After the game, Emlyn Hughes led his team on a lap of honour. Shankly did not accompany them but stood on the Wembley turf soaking in the euphoria around him because he knew this was going to be his last chance to taste success with a team of his creation.

As he stood taking in all the jubilation going on around him, a hugely symbolic event occurred: a couple of Liverpool fans who had made their way onto the pitch knelt down in reverence and kissed the Liverpool manager's feet. It was like a spontaneous act of homage to a religious messiah - to the two Koppites indeed it was - they knew why they did it and so did the many thousands of Liverpool fans who witnessed the scene. In their moment of elation, they had chosen not to run after the Liverpool team as they made their way around the stadium but went instead to the person who had made the magnificent display they had just witnessed possible: Bill Shankly. It was to him they paid homage on behalf of all Liverpool supporters. Speaking about the incident in his autobiography, Shankly claimed that it was a gesture of respect, not only to him but to the team and the way they had played. There can be little doubt that the Liverpool supporters held their team in the highest regard but their ultimate acclamation was for a sixty-year-old Scot; the man they idolized.

The following day, Liverpool paraded through the city, displaying the FA Cup to the thousands who lined the streets. Brian Hall remembers that Shankly looked deep in thought as he waved to the joyous fans from an open-topped bus. He asked Hall: *'Hey son, who's that Chinaman, you know, the one with the sayings? What's his name?'* Hall remembers looking at Shankly and thinking *'Are you barmy, or what?'* Hall replied *'Is it Chairman Mao you mean?'* Shankly became excited *'That's him son, that's the man.'*

Hall thought no more of Shankly's question until he arrived at St George's Hall, which was the final stop on their parade through the city. Hall recalls that there must have been more than 300,000 flocking around the old, Victorian building to hear speeches from civil dignitaries and their Liverpool heroes. Shankly came to the microphone and exclaimed: *'Chairman Mao could never have seen such a show of red strength.'* The crowd roared their approval. In an instant Shankly had summed up the situation and come up with the perfect response. Hall recalls thinking *'This man's a genius.'*

Liverpool FC parade around the streets of Liverpool with the FA Cup, 1974.

Retirement

WITH the Wembley display in mind, Liverpool supporters were confident that Shankly had created a team capable of staying at the top for many years to come. They could barely wait for the new season to begin. Like the rest of the football world, they listened with anticipation as a press conference was called at Anfield on July 12, 1974. Never a team to rest on its laurels, they expected to hear news of a major new signing for the new season. The announcement that Ray Kennedy would be joining Liverpool from Arsenal for £200,000 surprised them a little but they were always keen to see quality players added to their squad. However, when the Liverpool chairman, John Smith, read out his next statement, it sent half of Merseyside into shock:

It is with great regret that, as chairman of the board, I have to inform you that Mr Shankly has intimated to us that he wishes to retire from league football.

When the news of Shankly's decision spread around Merseyside there was a widespread feeling of disbelief. Since arriving at Anfield, Shankly had always joked at the end of each season that he would probably call it a day. It may have been Shankly's way of keeping the board on their toes but it was a threat they never expected him to carry out. *'It's just one of Bill's funny ways'* was the general feeling within the club. But this time it was for real and was a decision that Shankly would not reverse.

There was much speculation about the reasons behind Shankly's decision to retire. In his autobiography, Shankly revealed that he had been thinking about it for well over a year. He wanted to spend more time with his family and take a break from the relentless pressures of managing a First Division club. Joe Mercer, who had experienced at first hand the pressure of being a First Division manager once said:

Bill Shankly used so much nervous energy in building up Liverpool that it would have lit up the city for years if it turned into electricity!

Shankly was always a man who gave himself totally to whatever task he set himself and this type of dedication had obviously taken its toll on him, not

Above: Shankly waves to the Liverpool supporters at Wembley before the 1974 Charity Shield match.

Below: Shankly and Brian Clough lead out Liverpool and Leeds at Wembley before the 1974 Charity Shield match.

physically but mentally. Interviewed after announcing his retirement, Nessie Shankly, a woman with the same total honesty as her husband, stated:

Bill's as fit as a fiddle but you can be fit and still be tired. He gives so much of himself to the game. I've never really pushed him and I've always been behind any decisions he made. But last year I asked him to think about retirement and it is for me that he has announced his retirement.

Once Shankly had made a decision, there was never going to be any going back. He knew he was leaving the team and the club in a very strong position. With the team now managed by Bob Paisley, backed by Joe Fagan, Ronnie Moran, Roy Evans, Reuben Bennett and Tom Saunders, continuity was maintained and continued success on the playing front looked assured.

After his retirement, Shankly kept up his links with football, taking in as many fixtures as he could. Whatever club he visited, he was always given a great reception, particularly at Everton. It may have been relief that the Goodison regulars felt, knowing that there would be no more Shankly teams coming to Everton to do battle with the Blues. It is more likely, however, that the majority of Evertonians had great respect for the man who had given his all to football. Bryan Robson remembers Shankly once calling into the Manchester United dressing room before a match:

What impressed me was the way he went around every player. He was not one to deliver long sermons, they were little bits of advice. His manner and even his accent used to make me laugh and one of his great strengths was that he had the ability to tell a player off and crack a joke at the same time.

Shankly could be scathing at times but he chose his words so well, players found themselves being torn off a strip and walking away with a broad grin on their faces instead of hanging their heads in despair. Former Manchester United legend, George Best, also paid tribute to Shankly in his autobiography:

Bill Shankly, like Celtic's Jock Stein and Spurs' Bill Nicholson, was a manager who was able to mix and form a friendship with his players but he was also able to remain aloof from them. He was an honest man, a man of integrity.

Shankly began to pay regular Friday night visits across the Mersey to watch and give advice to Tranmere Rovers, who were managed by his friend and devotee, Johnny King. Indeed, it was Shankly who put the seal on Manchester United's signing of Steve Coppell from Tranmere. The future England star was recommended to the then United manager, Tommy Docherty, by Jimmy Murphy, who was a key figure at Old Trafford during the glory days of the

Opposite: Seen here at the press conference to announce his retirement from league football, 1974.

69

1950s and 60s. Always an astute judge of young soccer talent, Murphy watched the Tranmere youngster on just one occasion before telling Docherty to sign him. Knowing that Shankly was a regular visitor to Tranmere, Docherty phoned him at his home and asked for his opinion of Coppell. When Shankly confirmed Murphy's glowing assessment, Docherty signed the player, who turned out to be one of United's bargain buys of all time, without ever having seen him play.

Shankly also kept up his daily training routine and at first would travel regularly to Liverpool's training ground at Melwood to use the facilities. Understandably, the players who had still not become accustomed to the fact that Bob Paisley was now in charge and that Shankly had retired, would still welcome him with *'Good morning, Boss!'* Obviously, the club was keen for Paisley to be accepted quickly by the players as their new manager and a certain amount of animosity began to develop between Shankly and the club.

In fairness to Liverpool FC, they appeared to have been quietly confident that Shankly would retract his notice of resignation and the actual realisation that he would not be resuming the new season as manager seemed to have caught them by surprise as it did the rest of the football world.

The perfect scenario would have been for them to have lost no time in offering Shankly a directorship as an acknowledgement for his wonderful achievements for the club. Sadly in football, as in life in general, what appears a logical course of action often fails to materialise. Although it seems inconceivable that the club would have knowingly offended Shankly, the man who had built it into one of the world's top clubs, a rift developed and relations between the two parties soured. Shankly still attended Liverpool's home games but stopped going into the director's box, sitting in preference in the stand or on the Kop. He was spotted on the Kop during a November, 1975, game against Coventry and interviewed by the Liverpool Echo a few days later he declared:

When I was a boy I used to watch Celtic and Rangers play with 100,000 there, and that was nothing to us. The wheel had turned full circle. This time it was with a red and white scarf. I got it from a boy and brought it home. I am a citizen of Liverpool and I wanted to go there to see the fans who have done so much for me. The handshakes are real, they aren't false. It was an enjoyable experience, and not as tiring as you might think.

From all accounts, once the news of Shankly's presence spread around the Kop a chant went up: *'Shankly is our King, Shankly is our king!'* Perhaps his relationship with the club had deteriorated but to hear the people who meant more to him than anyone else in football chant his name and shake his hand meant it had all been worthwhile.

One thing that Shankly's retirement from management did not change was his love of playing football and, even though well into his sixties, he would still play every Sunday afternoon. The two teams would be made up of dads and kids with the match taking place in a park near his Liverpool home. Shankly, dressed in his all-red track suit, would throw himself into these games with the same energy and enthusiasm that had been a feature of his playing days at Preston.

Former Everton player, Mick Lyons, remembered meeting Shankly as the football-mad Scot was making his way home after his weekly game: *'Mick! Had a great game today, we won 19-17!'* exclaimed an excited Shankly, hardly able to contain himself after another enjoyable Sunday afternoon. Indeed, Shankly, who once remarked: *'When I die, I want people to walk past my coffin and say "Christ, there lies a fit man!",'* maintained such a high level of fitness that it seemed unimaginable to many that he would ever be susceptible to physical illness. The news of his sudden death on September 29, 1981, was met with shock and disbelief throughout Merseyside and the football world in general.

Farewell to Anfield. Shankly before his benefit match, 1975.

When the sense of grief began to lift, tributes began to pour in for the much loved Scot with the human touch, all of them genuine and heartfelt. Particularly poignant, and an example of how the death of Shankly saddened the whole of Merseyside, was a tribute from the leader of the Indian community in Liverpool. He recalled the occasion when Shankly was guest of honour at their Diwali celebrations: *'Don't forget that being a Scot I'm also an immigrant to Liverpool,'* he told his appreciative Hindu hosts during his brief speech.

In the football world, the loss of a man who had been like a second father to many of them, left his former Liverpool players devastated. Many of them had now moved into football management themselves and had always sought Shankly's guidance and advice in moments of need. All were quick to pay their respects to their former manager but their feelings were probably best summed up by Ian St John, who said:

Shanks was capable of exaggerating any situation to get the best out of players - it is impossible to exaggerate his loss.

Perhaps the most appropriate epitaph was written by Shankly himself in his autobiography when he wrote:

Above all, I would like to be remembered as a man who was selfless, who strove and worried so that others could share the glory, and who built up a family of people who could hold their heads up high and say 'We're Liverpool'.

Bill Shankly, the legend of Anfield, will certainly be remembered for all of these reasons and more, much more.

Bill Shankly O.B.E. with wife
Nessie, 1974.

The Great Motivator

THE secret of Shankly's managerial success owed a great deal to his ability to motivate. Practically every player who played under Shankly, whether it was in the Third Division at Carlisle and Workington, or in the First Division with Liverpool, claims that Shankly's ability to motivate was phenomenal. Every player that Shankly signed was told the same message: you're going to become a great player. Ron Yeats, recalling his initial period at Liverpool, once said:

I was a big lad, but when the Boss had finished even I felt bigger - I could have touched the roof of the Kop. To him we were each the best player in our respective positions in the history of the game and there wasn't a team in the world that could live with us - or so he had us believe. Having arrived from Scotland with a 'will I make it?' feeling and perhaps lacking in confidence, he made a fantastic difference to my game. Even I could sense the improvement in my play.

Shankly was also a master at pinpointing a player's strong points and weaknesses. Full-back Alec Lindsay was initially overawed when he first arrived at Liverpool from Bury and his confidence in his playing ability began to wain. Lindsay recalls that:

I was signed from Bury as a midfield player, but at first couldn't settle in. I was stripping alongside Roger Hunt and Peter Thompson and asking myself how the hell I had got there. I lost all my confidence and felt really down. But Shankly wasn't having any of that for long. He got me working at my game, at my fitness, and he worked at my confidence. Then, as I had played in the left side of defence on occasion at Bury, I was tried on the left-hand side of the back four - and I never looked back.

Lindsay went on to become an international player at this position.

Shankly also had the ability to spot the players who suffered from pre-match nerves and would quickly put them at their ease with just a few simple words. Emlyn Hughes recalled:

I've seen players sitting in the dressing room quaking with nerves. They could hear the roar of the crowd through the dressing room walls, they knew what a big job was in front of them, and they would just go to pieces. But then in walks Shanks, and before the player knows, he's feeling tremendous, like a new man. Once Shanks has turned on his 'magic', you'd go out and face any opposition - simply because, I think, you believed what Shanks said. Sometimes it might have been outrageous, but usually it was just sound, simple sense.

To Shankly the game and how to play it was simplicity itself. He never tried to complicate things in either training or playing and he scorned the new phraseology of modern day football. But in many ways, the tactics that the Shankly teams of the 1960s and early 70s employed were ahead of their time. He was probably the first manager to introduce a cover defender alongside the centre-half; which, in the successful 1960s team, tended to be Tommy Smith playing alongside Ron Yeats. Indeed, Shankly was reported to have explained the new role that he wanted Smith to play by telling him to think of himself of Ron Yeats's right leg! Shankly also coached his defenders to push up and his forwards to take up a midfield role when the opposition had the ball. This system reduced the space available to the opposition and would deny them time to play the ball. It was a system that most teams found hard to come to terms with and was the basis of much of Liverpool's success.

To play this system, however, Shankly's teams had to be superbly fit and Shankly would at times drive his players on relentlessly until the desired level of fitness was attained. Shankly would never ask his players to attempt a training activity that he would not have been able to accomplish himself during his playing days and when it came to five-a-side games, he demanded that his players did not hold back with the tackles on him as he played alongside them. It was also important to him that his players were given a lot of ball work in training. *'Joe Davies doesn't run around the snooker table.'* he once exclaimed, as he recalled the training methods of some clubs, who would simply run players around the playing area day after day with not a sight of the ball until match day. Pre-season road running at Anfield was also abolished by Shankly, who commented: *'You don't play on tarmac, you play on grass.'*

Shankly also changed the way that the youth players at Anfield were treated. Chris Lawler was a groundstaff boy at Anfield when Shankly arrived in 1959. His main tasks were to sweep the changing rooms and clean the first team players' boots. *'That's no good for you, you're going to be footballers.'* Shankly told Lawler and the other groundstaff teenagers. From then on the groundstaff boys trained with the first team and reserve players and only carried out their cleaning duties when the day's training was over.

Shankly deep in thought.

Perhaps the most well known of Shankly's motivational tactics was the way in which he vilified the opposition. Interviewed by the Liverpool Echo in the 1970s Bob Paisley recalled Shankly's pre-match team talks:

His personality was overwhelming. It was this terrific personality, his passion for the game, which enabled him to lift players. He did it by personality, not by tactical talks. He didn't have tactical talks at Anfield as most people understand them. Your opponents couldn't play. His favourite word was 'rubbish'. He would tell the Liverpool players that their opponents were rubbish and they were the greatest. It may sound silly, but it worked with Bill Shankly because of his personality. He made his players believe.

Tom Saunders, who was Youth Development Officer at Anfield during the Shankly years, was also privy to some of Shankly's pre-match talks and recalled one occasion when football was the last topic on the agenda:

The players waited for their instructions and Shankly began to speak and continued for some fifteen minutes. Not about the opposition or even football. Oh, no! Boxing was the sole subject for a quarter of an hour. He then switched to football but quickly brought the proceedings to a halt. 'Don't let's waste time! That bloody lot can't play at all.' With that, the team talk was rapidly brought to a close.

But Saunders had no doubts that Shankly's constant rubbishing of the opposition was a shrewd Shankly tactic that gave the Liverpool players an aura of invincibility that was worth a good start. On the odd occasion, however, Shankly would praise the opposition but once again it would be part of his ploy to boost his own players' self-esteem. Bob Paisley recalled Shankly praising one of their European opponents, Anderlecht, who boasted ten Belgian internationals in their team:

Before the game, in the dressing room, Bill talked to the lads. He said 'You've read about Anderlecht having all these internationals and how good they are. Forget it. They can't play. They're rubbish. I've seen them and I'm telling you. You'll murder them, so get out there and do it.' The boys went out there and murdered them. They won 3-0. And after the game, Bill burst into the dressing room and said, 'Boys, you've just beaten the greatest team in Europe.'

Because of the strength of his personality Shankly could tell his players one thing and then totally contradict what he had told them yet, somehow, they accepted it without question.

Another key factor in Shankly's managerial success was the incredible amount of time he invested in the game. Shankly would travel the length and breadth of Britain watching matches in his endless search for new talent. During his early days at Liverpool, he was known to have personally checked on over thirty centre-halves before deciding to sign Ron Yeats. Although Shankly liked nothing better than to be at home with his feet up watching television, his pursuit of success for Liverpool meant that he did not often get the chance to relax. Tommy Docherty, aware of the long hours that Shankly spent watching football around the country once remarked: *'If he'd been paid overtime, he'd have been a millionaire.'* But to Shankly, the long hours were all part of the job as he acknowledged in his autobiography:

I've been a slave to football. It follows you home, it follows you everywhere, and eats into your family life. But every working man misses out on some things because of his job.

To Shankly it was a price he was prepared to pay in his relentless drive to make Liverpool FC the greatest team in the land.

Wit And Wisdom

The quotes and anecdotes involving Bill Shankly are legendary and could fill a book on their own. Here is a selection of some of the most memorable ones.

Football is not a matter of life and death; it's much more important than that.

A lot of football success is in the mind. You must believe you are the best and then make sure you are. In my time at Liverpool, we always said we had the best two teams on Merseyside: Liverpool and Liverpool Reserves.

If you are first, you are first. If you are second, you are nothing.

The trouble with football referees is that they know the rules but they do not know the game.

Of course I didn't take my wife to see Rochdale as an anniversary present. It was her birthday. Would I have got married during the football season? And anyway, it wasn't Rochdale, it was Rochdale Reserves.

To a reporter in the 1960s: *Yes. Roger Hunt misses a few, but he gets in the right place to miss them.*

Shankly liked to tell the following story about the 1966 Everton v Sheffield Wednesday FA Cup Final: *Princess Margaret asked Everton captain, Brian Labone: 'Mr Labone, where is Everton?' Labone answered 'In Liverpool, Ma'am.' To which Princess Margaret replied, 'Of course, we had your first team here last year'.*

After signing Scottish giant, Ron Yeats, Shankly remarked: *With him in defence, we could play Arthur Askey in goal.*

After a hard fought 1-1 result, Shankly's post-match comment was: *The best side drew.*

When Liverpool were held to a 0-0 draw at Anfield, he commented: *What can you do, playing against eleven goalposts?*

80

Shankly once told a journalist who made the mistake of criticising his team selection: *Laddie, I never drop players, I only make changes.*

Explaining the 'This is Anfield' plaque in the Liverpool tunnel: *It reminds our players where they are... and it warns the opposition.*

To Shankly there was no finer stadium than Anfield and he once remarked on the pitch: *It's great grass at Anfield, professional grass.*

After the erection of a new stand at Anfield in 1971: *The ground is now fit for our great team and our wonderful supporters.*

After hearing that Celtic's Lou Macari had turned down Liverpool in favour of Manchester United, he covered his obvious dejection by telling his squad: *He couldn't play anyway. I only wanted him for the reserve team.*

Shankly was reputed to be the only manager of an English club at the famous Celtic v Inter Milan European Cup Final in Portugal in 1967. After Celtic became the first British team to win the trophy, he told his friend Jock Stein: *John, you're immortal now. Mind you, Liverpool would have beaten that lot!*

Jock Stein, himself a noted wit, once said: *I don't believe everything Bill tells me about his players. Had they been that good, they'd not only have won the European Cup but the Ryder Cup, the Boat Race and even the Grand National!*

On one of Liverpool's numerous European trips, he was filling in the hotel registration form, writing 'football' under occupation and 'Anfield' under address. *But, sir,* protested the receptionist, *you need to fill in where you live. Lady,* replied Shankly, *in Liverpool there is only one address that matters and that is where I live.*

Negotiating a transfer deal in his office, he was distracted by the noise of reporters having a kick about in the car park to pass time before the announcement. *What the hell,* he roared, *they can't play football. Bob, Reuben, Joe, Ronnie... get the strips and we'll play them five-a-side!*

During another five-a-side match at Melwood, Shankly scored a goal. When the other players insisted it was offside, he turned to Chris Lawler, one of the quietest members in the squad. *Was it a goal?* he demanded, *Was I offside? Yes, boss, you were,* Lawler replied. Shankly looked at him in utter disbelief: *Chris, you've been here for four years and have never said a word and when you do it's a bloody lie!*

Attending the funeral of Everton legend Dixie Dean, Shankly was amazed by the size of the crowd outside St James's Church. Shaking his head in wonderment, he remarked: *I know this is a sad occasion but I think that Dixie would have been amazed to know that even in death he could draw a bigger crowd than Everton can on a Saturday afternoon.*

When it was put to him that he did not have the experience of playing in an Everton/Liverpool derby match, unlike Everton manager Billy Bingham, he replied: *Nonsense! I've kicked every ball, headed out every cross. I once scored a hat-trick; one was lucky but the others were great goals.*

After the sensational defeat of Everton in the 1971 Cup semi-final he commented: *Sickness would not have kept me away from this one. If I'd been dead, I would have had them bring the casket to the ground, prop it up in the stands and cut a hole in the lid.*

During the 1960s, when Liverpool and Everton rivalry was intense, Shankly still found time to ring up Everton's Alan Ball, a player he greatly admired, to talk football. Alan Ball once remarked: *Shankly was very special. The greatness of the man was the fact that he wasn't frightened to give praise, even if it was to the so-called worst enemy.'*

Shankly was famed for his telephone calls to other managers. Bill Nicholson, the great Spurs manager, recalls a Sunday morning call: *After the usual hellos, I mentioned Liverpool's 2-0 defeat the previous day. Quick as a flash, Bill growled, 'No, no, Billy... we murdered them, we were all over them. The first wasn't a goal at all and the second, well, you've never seen anything like it.'*

Don Revie regularly received a Sunday morning call. Each followed the same ritual, with Shankly eulogising over his Liverpool players. Every player would be praised, including the substitute who would have contributed to the victory even if he had not played. To Shankly every player in that red strip had everything: a right foot, left foot, tackling, heading and stamina. No player had a weakness, they were each the best player, position for position in the world. When Revie managed to get in a mention of one of his own players, Shankly would just say, *a fair player, nae bad*, leaving Revie wondering how Leeds ever managed to win a match with no great players, not even good ones for all that Bill would admit to.

Barry Farrell, the photographer, once asked Shankly whether he thought Brian Clough's outspokenness was doing him a disservice. *Laddie,* retorted an annoyed Shankly, *that man scored some two hundred goals in two hundred* and seventy matches - an incredible record - and he has won cup after cup as a manager. When he talks, pin back your ears.

Football and boxing were his two great loves but football always came first. Alan Rudkin offered Shankly tickets for his title fight with Walter McGovern, which were accepted enthusiastically. However, on the morning of the fight Rudkin received a telephone call: *Alan, I'm sorry but I can't make it. There's a schoolboy match I want to see.*

Rudkin also remembered hosting a meeting of Liverpool fans from London at Anfield. Shankly entered the room and turned to one awe-struck fan. *Where are you from?* Nervously the boy answered, *I'm a Liverpool fan from London. Well, laddie... what's it like to be in heaven?*

Right up until his last day with Liverpool Shankly was full of wit and humour. Just before his retirement was announced, television crews had arrived and began switching on the lights. *Hold it a minute,* he called out, *John Wayne hasn't arrived yet.*

Having made his retirement speech, he left to sign Ray Kennedy from Arsenal with a parting comment: *There'll not be many days like this.*

A Lifetime's Record

SHANKLY'S RECORD AS A PLAYER

Cronberry Juniors, Scottish Junior League 1930-32

Carlisle United, Division Three North, Joined July 1932
Debut December 31, 1932 v Rochdale
Appeared in 16 league games

Preston North End, Division Two, Joined July 1933
Debut December 9, 1933 v Hull City, Won 5-0 (home)
1st League goal: v Liverpool, February 2, 1938
Final game: v Sunderland, March 19, 1949 (home)
League appearences: 297
Scored: 13 league goals (8 penalties)
Honours:
1933-34 Runners-up Division Two
1936-37 FA Cup Runners-up
1937-38 FA Cup Winners

INTERNATIONAL RECORD FOR SCOTLAND
1938 v England
1939 v England
1939 v Wales
1939 v Northern Ireland
1939 v Hungary

WARTIME HONOURS
Seven wartime international caps.
1940-41 Played for Preston North End when they won the North Regional
League Championship.
1940-41 Played for Preston in their successful wartime League Cup
Final victory over Arsenal. Preston won after a replay.
Shankly created a football league record when he played 43
successive FA Cup ties for one club: Preston North End.
RAF representative honours in football and boxing.

MANAGERIAL CAREER

Carlisle

Joined March 1949, first game in charge April 9

Season	Played	Won	Drew	Lost	Final League Position
1948-49	7	1	4	2	15th Division 3 North
1949-50	42	16	15	11	9th Division 3 North
1950-51	46	25	12	9	3rd Division 3 North

Grimsby

Joined July 1951

Season	Played	Won	Drew	Lost	Final League Position
1951-52	46	29	8	9	2nd Division 3 North
1952-53	46	22	9	15	5th Division 3 North
1953-54*	26	11	4	11	(17th Division 3 North)

*Shankly resigned on January 2, 1954

Workington

Became manager January 6, 1954

Season	Played	Won	Drew	Lost	Final League Position
1953-54	20	8	6	6	18th Division 3 North
1954-55	46	18	14	14	8th Division 3 North
1955-56*	19	9	3	7	-

*Shankly resigned on November 15, 1955

Huddersfield

Joined December 10, 1955, became manager November 5, 1956

Season	Played	Won	Drew	Lost	Final League Position
1956-57	26	11	4	11	12th Division 2
1957-58	42	14	16	12	9th Division 2
1958-59	42	16	8	18	14th Division 2
1959-60*	19	8	5	6	(6th Division 2)

*Shankly resigned on December 1, 1959

Liverpool

Joined December 1959, first game in charge December 19

Season	Played	Won	Drew	Lost	Final League Position	
1959-60	21	11	5	5	3rd	Division 2
1960-61	42	21	10	11	3rd	Division 2
1961-62	42	27	8	7	1st	Division 2
1962-63	42	17	10	15	8th	Division 1
1963-64	42	26	5	11	1st	Division 1
1964-65	42	17	10	15	7th	Division 1
1965-66	42	26	9	7	1st	Division 1
1966-67	42	19	13	10	5th	Division 1
1967-68	42	22	11	9	3rd	Division 1
1968-69	42	25	11	6	2nd	Division 1
1969-70	42	20	11	11	5th	Division 1
1970-71	42	17	17	8	5th	Division 1
1971-72	42	24	9	9	3rd	Division 1
1972-73	42	25	10	7	1st	Division 1
1973-74	42	22	13	7	2nd	Division 1

Honours as Liverpool Manager

1961-62	Champions Division Two
1962-63	FA Cup semi-finalists
1963-64	Champions Division One
1964-65	FA Cup winners
	European Cup semi-finalists
1965-66	Champions Division One
	European Cup Winners' Cup runners-up
1970-71	FA Cup runners-up
	European Cup Winners' Cup semi-finalists
1972-73	Champions Division One
	UEFA Cup winners
	Manager Of The Year trophy
1973-74	FA Cup winners

The Shankly Signings

WITH the possible exception of Kevin Keegan and Larry Lloyd, all of the Shankly signings were re-sold with their best playing years well behind them. Yet he still managed to show a net profit of well over half a million pounds (still a substantial sum in the 1970s). The lessons he learnt running a tight financial ship during his formative managerial years at Carlisle, Grimsby and Workington stayed with him for the rest of his career. Although not afraid to splash out on players when the situation demanded it, the profit figures show what a shrewd financial brain Shankly had.

1960 Sammy Reid, Winger £8,000 Motherwell

1960 Kevin Lewis, Winger £13,000 Sheffield United
1963 Huddersfield Town £18,000

1960 Gordon Milne, Midfield £16,000
1967 Blackpool £30,000

1961 Ian St John, Striker £37,500 Motherwell
1971 Coventry City No Fee

1961 Ron Yeats, Centre-half £30,000 Dundee United
1971 Tranmere Rovers No Fee

1961 Jim Furnell, Goalkeeper £18,000 Burnley
1964 Arsenal £15,000

1962 Willie Stevenson, Midfield £20,000 Rangers
1968 Stoke City £48,000

1963 Peter Thompson, Winger £32,000 Preston North End
1974 Bolton Wanderers £18,000

1964 Geoff Strong, Utility £40,000 Arsenal
1970 Coventry City £30,000

1964 Phil Chisnall, Striker £25,000 Manchester United
1967 Southend United £12,000

1965 John Ogston, Goalkeeper £10,000 Aberdeen
1968 Doncaster Rovers £2,500

1966 Stuart Mason, Full-back £20,000 Wrexham
1968 Wrexham No Fee

1966 Peter Wall, Full-back £6,000 Wrexham
1970 Crystal Palace £35,000

1966 Dave Wilson, Winger £20,000 Preston North End
1968 Preston North End £4,000

1966 Emlyn Hughes, Defence/Midfield £65,000 Blackpool
1979 Wolverhampton Wanderers £90,000

1967 Tony Hateley, Striker £96,000 Chelsea
1969 Coventry City £80,000

1968 Alun Evans, Striker £100,000 Wolverhampton Wanderers
1972 Aston Villa £70,000

1968 Ray Clemence, Goalkeeper £18,000 Scunthorpe
1981 Tottenham Hotspur £300,000

1969 Alec Lindsay, Full-back £68,000 Bury
1977 Stoke City £20,000

1969 Larry Lloyd, Centre-half £50,000 Bristol Rovers
1974 Coventry City £225,000

1970 Jack Whitham, Striker £57,000 Sheffield Wednesday
1974 Cardiff City No Fee

1970 Steve Heighway, Winger, No Fee Skelmersdale
1981 Minnesota Kicks No Fee

1970 John Toshack, Striker £110,000 Cardiff City
1978 Swansea City No Fee

1971 Kevin Keegan, Striker £35,000 Scunthorpe
1977 SV Hamburg £500,000

1972 Trevor Storton, Centre-half £25,000 Tranmere Rovers
1974 Chester City £18,000

1972 Frank Lane, Goalkeeper £15,000 Tranmere Rovers
1975 Notts County No Fee

1972 Peter Cormack, Midfield £110,000 Nottingham Forest
1976 Bristol City £50,000

1973 Alan Waddle, Striker £40,000 Halifax Town
1977 Leicester City £45,000

1974 Ray Kennedy, Striker/Midfield £200,000 Arsenal
1982 Swansea City £160,000

The Shankly Players

The following is a full list of the players who appeared for Liverpool during the Shankly era at Anfield, not including the Charity Shield.

A=Appearances S=Substitutions G=Goals

Player	League			FA Cup			L/Milk			Europe			Total		
	A	S	G	A	S	G	A	S	G	A	S	G	A	S	G
Alan A'Court	119	0	20	9	0	1	2	0	0	0	0	0	130	0	21
Alan Arnell	1	0	0	0	0	0	0	0	0	0	0	0	1	0	0
Steve Arnold	1	0	0	0	0	0	0	0	0	0	0	0	1	0	0
Alf Arrowsmith	43	4	20	6	0	4	0	0	0	1	0	0	50	4	24
Alan Banks	5	0	4	0	0	0	0	0	0	0	0	0	5	0	4
Reg Blore	1	0	0	0	0	0	0	0	0	0	0	0	1	0	0
Phil Boersma	52	6	11	7	3	1	2	2	2	9	5	6	70	16	20
Derek Brownbill	1	0	0	0	0	0	0	0	0	0	0	0	1	0	0
Gerry Byrne	273	1	2	29	0	0	5	0	0	22	0	1	329	1	3
Ian Callaghan	673	3	50	77	1	2	42	0	7	87	1	10	843	5	69
Bobby Campbell	14	0	1	0	0	0	0	0	0	0	0	0	14	0	1
Willie Carlin	1	0	0	0	0	0	0	0	0	0	0	0	1	0	0
Phil Chisnall	6	0	1	0	0	0	0	0	0	2	0	1	8	0	2
Ray Clemence	180	0	0	24	0	0	20	0	0	32	0	0	256	0	0
Peter Cormack	70	2	17	12	0	2	14	0	1	11	0	1	107	2	21
Alun Evans	77	2	21	9	2	3	7	0	2	11	2	7	104	6	33
Roy Evans	9	0	0	0	0	0	1	0	0	1	0	0	11	0	0
Chris Fagan	1	0	0	0	0	0	0	0	0	0	0	0	1	0	0
Phil Fearns	27	0	1	1	0	0	0	0	0	0	0	0	28	0	1
Jim Furnell	28	0	0	0	0	0	0	0	0	0	0	0	28	0	0
Bobby Graham	96	5	31	7	2	4	7	1	2	13	0	5	123	8	42
Brian Hall	93	14	8	15	1	3	7	1	1	17	5	2	132	19	14
Jimmy Harrower	34	0	10	3	0	1	3	0	0	0	0	0	40	0	11
Tony Hately	42	0	17	7	0	8	2	0	0	5	0	3	56	0	28
Steve Heighway	142	3	20	19	0	4	19	0	5	27	0	4	207	3	33
Dave Hickson	54	0	32	4	0	0	3	0	1	0	0	0	61	0	33
Alan Hignet	1	0	0	0	0	0	0	0	0	0	0	0	1	0	0
Emlyn Hughes	294	0	31	42	0	1	27	0	3	42	0	7	405	0	44
Roger Hunt	386	3	237	44	0	18	10	0	5	29	2	17	469	5	277
Alan Jones	5	0	0	0	0	0	0	0	0	0	0	0	5	0	0
Kevin Keegan	219	0	34	16	0	8	15	0	6	18	0	4	167	0	52
Frank Lane	1	0	0	0	0	0	1	0	0	0	0	0	2	0	0

Player	League			FA Cup			L/Milk			Europe			Total		
	A	S	G	A	S	G	A	S	G	A	S	G	A	S	G
Chris Lawler	396	0	41	47	0	4	24	0	5	62	0	11	529	0	61
Tommy Lawrence	306	0	0	42	0	0	6	0	0	33	0	0	387	0	0
Tommy Leishman	107	0	6	9	0	0	3	0	1	0	0	0	119	0	7
Kevin Lewis	71	0	39	8	0	3	2	0	0	0	0	0	81	0	44
Billy Liddell	12	0	1	0	0	0	0	0	0	0	0	0	12	0	1
Alec Lindsay	136	2	9	20	0	1	16	0	0	25	0	3	197	0	13
Doug Livermore	13	3	0	0	0	0	1	0	0	0	0	0	14	3	0
Larry Lloyd	150	0	4	16	0	0	20	0	0	31	0	1	217	0	5
Tom Lowry	1	0	0	0	0	0	0	0	0	0	0	0	1	0	0
John McLaughlin	38	2	2	4	0	1	3	0	0	8	0	0	53	2	3
Jimmy Melia	144	0	28	15	0	2	0	0	0	0	0	0	159	0	30
Gordon Milne	234	2	18	27	0	1	0	0	0	16	0	0	277	2	19
Bill Molyneux	1	0	0	0	0	0	0	0	0	0	0	0	1	0	0
John Molyneux	86	0	1	5	0	0	3	0	0	0	0	0	94	0	1
Ronnie Moran	131	0	10	15	0	2	0	0	0	4	0	0	150	0	10
Fred Morris	1	0	0	0	0	0	0	0	0	0	0	0	1	0	0
Johnny Morrissey	23	0	5	1	0	0	0	0	0	0	0	0	24	0	5
John Ogston	1	0	0	0	0	0	0	0	0	0	0	0	1	0	0
Steve Peplow	2	0	0	0	0	0	0	0	0	1	0	0	3	0	0
Ian Ross	42	6	2	9	1	1	3	0	0	5	2	1	59	9	4
Dave Rylands	0	0	0	1	0	0	0	0	0	0	0	0	1	0	0
John Sealey	1	0	1	0	0	0	0	0	0	0	0	0	1	0	1
Bert Slater	99	0	0	9	0	0	3	0	0	0	0	0	111	0	0
Tommy Smith	369	0	32	46	0	2	20	0	2	63	1	6	498	1	42
Willie Stevenson	188	0	15	24	0	1	0	0	0	25	1	0	237	1	17
Ian St John	334	2	95	49	1	12	6	0	1	30	2	10	419	5	118
Trevor Storton	5	0	0	1	0	0	4	0	0	1	1	0	11	1	0
Geoff Strong	150	5	29	23	0	1	4	0	0	16	0	2	193	5	32
Bobby Thompson	6	0	0	1	0	0	0	0	0	0	0	0	7	0	0
Max Thompson	1	0	0	0	0	0	0	0	0	0	1	0	1	1	0
Peter Thompson	318	4	41	37	1	5	9	0	2	40	3	6	404	8	54
Phil Thompson	47	3	0	11	0	0	4	1	0	4	2	0	66	6	0
John Toshack	90	1	36	18	0	6	9	0	3	15	3	3	132	4	48
Alan Waddle	11	5	1	2	0	0	3	0	0	0	1	0	16	6	1
Peter Wall	31	0	0	6	0	0	2	0	0	3	0	0	42	0	0
Gordon Wallace	19	1	3	0	0	0	0	0	0	1	0	2	20	1	5
Johnny Wheeler	46	0	5	3	0	1	3	0	0	0	0	0	52	0	6
Dick White	87	0	0	5	0	0	3	0	0	0	0	0	95	0	0
Jack Whitham	15	0	7	0	0	0	1	0	0	0	0	0	16	0	7
Dave Wilson	0	1	0	0	0	0	0	0	0	0	0	0	0	1	0
Ron Yeats	357	1	13	50	0	0	7	0	0	36	0	2	450	1	15

Bibliography

George Best & Ross Benson,
The Good, the Bad and the Bubbly: The Autobiography,
Pan Books, 1991.

Ronald Cowing, Martin Lawson & Bill Willcox,
The Carlisle United Story,
Lakeside Publications, 1974.

Ted Croker,
The First Voice You Will Hear Is - An Autobiography,
Willow Books, 1987.

Eamon Dunphy,
A Strange Kind of Glory: Sir Matt Busby and Manchester United,
Heinemann, 1991.

Roddy Forsyth,
The Only Game: The Scots and World Football,
Mainstream Publishing Company, 1990.

Terry Frost,
Huddersfield Town: A Complete Record 1910-1990,
Breedon Books, 1990.

John Gibson,
Kevin Keegan: Portrait of a Superstar,
Comet WH Allen, London, 1984.

Matthew Graham,
Liverpool,
Hamlyn, 1984.

Ian Hargraves,
Liverpool Greats,
Sports Print Publishing in Association with The Liverpool Echo, 1989.

Ian Hargraves, Ken Rogers & Ric George,
Liverpool Club of the Century,
Liverpool Echo Publication, 1988.

Graham Hart (Ed.),
The Guinness Football Encyclopedia,
Guinness Publishing, 1991.

Steve Heighway,
Liverpool: My Team,
Souvenir Press, 1977.

Derek Hodgson,
The Liverpool Story,
Arthur Barker, 1978.

Arthur Hopcraft,
The Football Man: People and Passions in Soccer,
Sports Pages, Simon & Schuster, 1988.

Roger Hunt,
Hunt For Goals,
Pelham Books, 1969.

Frank Keating,
Long Days, Late Nights,
Robson Books Ltd, 1984.

Kevin Keegan & John Roberts,
Kevin Keegan,
Arthur Barker, 1977.

Stephen F. Kelly,
You'll Never Walk Alone: The Official Illustrated History of Liverpool FC,
Macdonald Queen Anne Press, 1987.

Doug Lamming,
Who's Who of Liverpool 1892-1989,
Breedon Books, 1989.

Mark Lawrenson,
Mark Lawrenson: The Autobiography,
Queen Anne Press, 1988.

Stan Liversedge,
Liverpool 1892-1992: The Official Centenary History,
Hamlyn, 1991.

Brian Pead,
Liverpool Champions of Champions,
Breedon Books, 1990.

Ivan Ponting,
Liverpool Player by Player,
The Crowood Press, 1990.

Bryan Robson,
Bryan Robson Glory, Glory Man United,
Collins/Willow, 1992.

Johnny Rogan,
The Football Managers,
Macdonald and Queen Anne Press, 1989.

Ken Rogers,
Everton Greats,
Sports Print Publishing in Association with The Liverpool Echo, 1989.

Jack Rollin,
Soccer at War, 1939-45,
Willow Books, Collins, 1985.

A Legend in his own time,
David Glyn Associates, Chester, 1974.

Bill Shankly & John Roberts,
Shankly by Bill Shankly,
Arthur Barker, 1976.

Gerald Sinstadt & Brian Barwick,
The Great 1962-88 Derbies: Everton v Liverpool,
BBC Books, 1988.

Ian St John & Jimmy Greaves,
Football is a Funny Old Game,
Stanley Paul & Co. Ltd, 1986.

John Toshack,
Tosh: An Autobiography,
Arthur Barker Ltd, 1982.

Les Triggs, David Hepton & Sid Woodhead,
Grimsby Town: A Complete Record 1878-1989,
Breedon Books, 1989.

John Williams & Stephen Wagg (Eds.),
British Football and Social Change: Getting into Europe,
Leicester University Press, 1991.

Martin Wingfield,
So Sad, So Very Sad...The League History of Workington AFC,
Worthing Typesetting, 1992

Special Thanks

Don Cooper
Bryan Horsnell
Simon Marland
Roger Wash
Ted Griffith
Ken Rogers
Sid Woodhead
Jim Finney
Kevan Platt
Ian Rigby
Neil Farnworth

Douglas Lamming
Alan Jackson
Robert Reid
Martin Wingfield
Tommy Smith
Mike Davage
Katrina Ward
Ian Thomas
Peter Donald
David Steele

The Liverpool Daily Post and Echo Ltd
The Huddersfield Examiner
Kirklees Photographic Archive
The Glasgow Herald
The Lancashire Evening Post

Huddersfield Town FC
Arsenal FC
Partick Thistle FC
Bolton Wanderers FC
Preston North End FC
Cardiff City FC
Norwich City FC
Luton Town FC
Grimsby Town FC
Workington FC